Princeton St

Jesse Lynch Williams

Alpha Editions

This edition published in 2024

ISBN 9789362094889

Design and Setting By
Alpha Editions
www.alphaedis.com
Email - info@alphaedis.com

Contents

THE WINNING OF THE CANE

The modern Cane Spree is held in broad daylight on University Field. It is a vastly different affair from the Spree we used to watch with chattering teeth at midnight, kneeling on the wet grass in front of Witherspoon, with a full moon watching over West College and Mat. Goldie and two assistants waiting by the lamp-post to join in the fierce rush which followed each bout.

Nowadays it is one of the regular events of the Annual Fall Handicap Games, and is advertised in large special feature letters on the posters hanging in the shop windows and on the bulletin elm. It is a perfectly proper and legitimate proceeding, and is watched like any other field event from the bleachers and Grand Stand, with girls there to catch their breath and say "Oh!" The class that wins is glad. They cheer awhile and then watch the final heat of the 2.20.

In our day you could seldom see much of anything, and there was nothing proper about it. But it was one of the things a fellow lived 4 for, like Thanksgiving games and Spring Term. To win a cane for one's class was an honor of a lifetime, like playing on the 'Varsity, or winning the Lynde debate. Men are still pointed out when back at Commencement as the light or middle weight spreers of their class, and a member of the faculty is famous for having "described a parabola with his opponent." This trick and a book called "Basal Concepts in Philosophy" bear his name, though it is maintained by some that he is more proud of the book.

This is to be a story of "How we used to do when we were in college." It would not do to revive the ancient cane spree. Things have changed since then. We are a university now. We mustn't behave like a college any longer. Besides, it was bad for the football men and training hours. But all the same, those old times were fun while they lasted. Weren't they?

High up over Clio Hall hung a moon, which a night or two before had been full. Over there, on the balconies of Witherspoon, blue and red and green lights were flaring. On the grass-plot in front was a huge black circle. This was made up of the College of New Jersey.

Their hats were off, and the red and the green and the blue mingled with the moonlight and glared upon the bare heads and the white of the faces with an effect as ghastly as it sounds.

The elms over toward Reunion and West cast long ugly-looking shadows. Beyond these everything seemed far away and dark and silent. Yet only a few hours before this same spot had served the innocent purpose of batting up flies and kicking footballs for points, with fellows shouting in loud, careless voices, "Aw! Come off! That was over the line!"

The circle was not yet perfectly formed. The crowd shivered and fidgeted, and borrowed lights of one another. Those behind called "Down in front!" And everyone wished it would begin. Some fellows kept edging in and were shoved back again by those appointed for that purpose. A few were moving about inside the circle displaying rolls of bills with which they made bets, and a great impression on under-classmen of a certain sort. The night was to be clear and frosty, and the strain on the nerves tremendous. So all those who believed in artificial warmth had it in their pockets, and some who did not.

For a month it had been, next to football, the most discussed topic at dinner-tables. Almost as soon as the rush was over—the annual cannon rush of the second night of the term without which the freshmen would not have considered themselves a class, while the underclassmen were still occupied in hazing and being hazed, and putting up and pulling down each other's proclamations throughout the state, and painting and repainting water-towers, and losing sleep in other good causes; in short, early in the term the candidates for the spreeing positions went into training, and they had been spreeing vigorously every night since—the freshmen back of the chapel and the sophs on the South Campus, about where Brown Hall now stands.

All sorts of rumors and counter-rumors had floated about the campus. The sophomores were frightened about a hinted-at dark horse of the freshmen, only they did not show it; and the freshmen were scared to death at the confident air of the well-known champion of the sophomores, and tried not to show it. And each was awed at the mysterious air of the other, and both had betted more than they had any business to on the result, and were now lined up in front of Witherspoon. All were as excited as they cared to be, and they had been cheering for themselves since nine o'clock. The cheers echoed in the frosty air from dark West and bright Witherspoon, and from far away first Church.

The sophomores were closely massed in the segment of the circle on the higher ground toward Reunion. Their cheering sounded blatant, and to the freshmen sickeningly confident. And the freshmen—they were opposite, with their sweet scared faces still more closely huddled together. Each freshman had his little cap safely tucked away in his innermost pocket, and none of them was saying a word, except when he opened his mouth to cheer with all his heart for his dear class. It was all new to them. They only waited and waited with the same aching suspense that you had on Thanksgiving-day, when you saw the referee toss the coin and one team take the ball while the other crouched, and then waited and waited, and you felt certain that something awful was the matter, but you did not know what.

Presently, though no official sign was given, every one felt that the important moment was at hand. The cheering sounded as if reinforcements had arrived. A compact circle was now formed by composite consent. Those in the front row sat down on the grass and caught cold. The next row kneeled. Those behind leaned on them, and so on back to those who stood on tip-toe and craned their necks for an occasional glimpse. Outside the circle, over by the Witherspoon lamp-post, leaned Proctor Matthew Goldie, Esquire, in a careless attitude.

Everyone's heart jumped up a little when a voice cried, "Here they come!" as though it were he who had to spree.

Led by their coachers, the two light weights scudded out mysteriously from different wings of Witherspoon with overcoats wrapped about them. As they crossed the light, the crowd, which had hushed for a moment, broke out in wild prolonged cheering; the two upper classes, who were not immediately interested, joined in. So did the sporting gentlemen of the town, and even the little muckers cheered shrilly for their favorite class.

A path was forced through the crowd, and the two nimble light weights began peeling their sweaters. The sophomore was dressed in black, the freshman in pure white. They resined their hands. Everyone felt things.

The referee held out the stout piece of hickory called cane by courtesy. He put the freshman's hands outside. The cheering ceased. Mat. Goldie stretched and changed his position.

There was a hurting stillness as they stood there with their feet braced, frozen in the ghastly glare, the one in white and the one in black, while the referee said, in earnest tones, "Are you ready, freshman?"

You could see his chest filling up from the bottom as he answered, "Um."

"Are you ready, sophomore?"

"Yes."

"Spree!"

One of them dropped as if shot, the other followed him down, both turned over, each began struggling and straining; the coachers began coaching, the referee dropped down on his knees to see fair play, and then someone in the rear said, "Down in front!" in healthy, human tones, and you came to yourself and remembered that this was only a struggle for class honor, after all, and that whichever way it came out it was not going to kill you. Then you breathed.

Meanwhile, locked up in a room in East Middle Witherspoon, wrapped in sweaters and blankets, were five other freshmen, and to them the strain was worst of all. These were the other freshmen spreers, the light weight, the middle weight, and the three substitutes. They could only wait and listen and try to guess from the sound of the cheers which side had the advantage. It was too far off to distinguish anything but a ring with something undefined inside. The juniors said they must not go out on the balcony or get excited. This was easy to say.

While the crowd was in the room and fellows were clattering up and down the stairs and everyone was talking and the crowd outside was making a noise, it was not so bad. But now it was so silent they could almost hear the two contestants straining and wrenching below. Now and then the shrill, earnest voice of a coacher would cut through the silence. "Now! Now!" with an echo from the Presbyterian Church. "Right over with him. Remember what I told you." Once the middle weight arose from the divan; then he sat down again. A little later one of the subs whistled two bars of a tune and stopped as if he had forgotten something. Once in a while someone glanced at one of the others and then looked away again. They did not say much.

The only one who did not seem to mind it was Hill, the substitute heavy weight, and that was only because he had not sense enough. He was a big, thick-headed, sleepy-looking farmer, and the only reason he was up here with these nimble athletes was that he was such a tremendous buck and so stupid that when once he put his big hands on the stick he would not let go. But he would be used only in case the regular heavy weight died or had a fit or something before time was called, and that was improbable.

But Hill was enjoying everything. He thought the colored lights were "pretty," and he considered it good fun, loafing in this large, luxurious room. He glanced approvingly at the water-colors and examined the photographs and knocked down a few of them, and looked over the mugs and the foils and the antlers and the usual dust collectors of a well-furnished room. Then, because he approved of what he saw, he grinned.

He had grinned at the staring crowd when, half an hour before, it had stood to one side for him and the other spreers to pass by on the way back from weighing at the gymnasium. He thought lots of things were funny. He grinned broadly when, before the spree began, an excitable junior approached him in the corner where he was sitting alone and said, in jerky, tremulous tones, "Say, which do you think will win?" This was before the crowd was put out. That was the funniest thing of all—the way Cunningham put the crowd out. "Dash it! I wish to dash you fellows would dash quickly get to dash out of here. This is my room and, dash it all, I loaned it to the dash freshmen spreers and not to the whole dash college, dash it!" That was so funny that Hill let loose his huge laugh and filled up the room with it. This caused the other freshmen to look at one another and smile pityingly. But Hill did not notice it.

The other freshmen had little in common with Hill. It was not so much because he was uncouth as that he had no class spirit. He had entered college two days late, and those two days are like two years in some respects. He had missed the class meeting, where freshmen get a first sight of one another which lasts always, and he had missed the class rush about the cannon, where freshmen are so closely pressed together that they never after get quite apart. But the farmer should have wakened up by this time. Lack of class spirit is never pardonable. This is the way Hill happened to be here this evening.

One day early in the term, as he was pushing his big chest across the campus to recitation, he heard someone call: "Hold up, there, you big freshman!" So he smiled and took off his ugly derby hat.

"No, I'm not a sophomore; I'm a junior," said the stranger, who then explained that he wanted to talk to him. "You come to my room at one o'clock, and don't forget about it," said the junior. "Run along, now; the bell is stopping."

Hill came, and found several other freshmen there. "Take hold of this stick," said the junior.

He put his big fists about it and found himself flying across the room. He landed against the door and beside him lay a table, which never arose.

"Now, that is cane-spreeing," said the junior casually, as one would say, "Down there is the new Art building," "and I want all you fellows to meet me at eight o'clock back of chapel."

That night they gave Hill a cane and said, "Take hold of this and don't let go." He held it for an hour against every one except the junior that was sophomore heavy weight the previous year. But he had never yet been quick enough to take it away from anyone, even the light weights. And that was the reason he was a substitute waiting in Montie Cunningham's room wrapped in two sweaters and a blanket. His eyes were closed and he was thinking about what a bully time his younger brother Ike must be having among the chestnuts this month.

The big leather chair was soft and he might have fallen asleep had not at that moment a tremendous yell burst into existence down below—a loud, shrill, fiendish yell which lasted nearly a minute before it was shaken down to an organized cheer. Hill stretched.

The others were out on the balcony. "Tell us which has it! For heaven's sake, tell us!" they cried to every one below; and no one below answered. So all they could do was to bite their lips and wait until the yelling became cheering, and then they knew from the exultant tones of the sophomores what they did not want to know.

Just then they caught a glimpse of the victor waving the cane in his hand as he was borne high on the shoulders of his class-mates to West Witherspoon.

Then they had a confused view of the rush. The upper classes fell to one side and the other two fell upon one another. This was the fiercest sort of rushing known to the proctors. The two sides were not, as in the cannon rush, evenly lined up four abreast. Not a bit of it. There were two thickly massed bodies of men, one running up a grade, the other charging down, and the roll of their footsteps was as the sound of much cattle, running. For a moment each tried to keep in solid form. But only long enough for some one to be knocked down and run over by the rest. After the first crash it was mixed fighting. In the moonlight one could not invariably distinguish friend from foe. So each man doubled up both fists and let drive at everyone he saw. It was glorious.

As soon as they became hopelessly mixed and each class had cheered itself hoarse and the proctors had carried off an armful of sophomores to appear before the Discipline Committee the next day, and to be cheered off at the depot by lamenting classmates later on, everyone turned up his coat-collar and helped form the ring again.

Those on the balcony, who had been panting and chafing like tied deer-hounds, now heard the feet of them bearing bad tidings and the defeated freshman up the entry stairs. The door was kicked open and three winded juniors laid their burden gently on the bed, which had been dragged in from the other room for this purpose. With them many others pushed in who did not belong there, and the room was full of people once more. Many voices were explaining how it all happened.

Ramsay, the little freshman, was completely done. He had fainted as they brought him upstairs. His face was set and white, and he lay there with his tough little resiny hands hanging limp at his side while his classmates poured brandy down his throat and told each other what to do. Through the window came a sharp freshman cheer with "Runt Ramsay" on the end.

Meanwhile the middle weight had stripped to the waist. He was bending forward with his forearms upon the mantel-piece and his forehead resting on them, as one bows during prayers in chapel. Two men were vigorously rubbing his long strong back with whiskey. The coach was standing beside him, giving final admonitions in a quick, tense manner. "Now, if he does this, you do this. See? He can't get you on that shoulder-throw of his. And if he tries this trick you know how to meet it. Why, you can do him dead easy. I won from him last year, and you can take it away from me," and so on. As they started from the room, he added, "Now remember your whole class is watching you and———" But the door closed and they hurried down the stairs, and in a moment the wild cheering announced their entrance in the ring. Hill was sorry, because he thought it right funny.

He went out on the balcony and looked down on the crowd. The noise and the moonlight and the specks of cigarlight had a grotesque effect. He had never seen anything like it before.

"Oh, cork up that laugh, Farmer Hill," said Bushforth, the heavy weight, who was also centre of the freshman team and had a right to patronize. "It's bad enough as it is, without that bark of yours."

Hill stopped laughing. He grinned instead. His feelings were not hurt. He had none.

Again the cheering was hushed. It was so still that those on the balcony might have heard the hard breathing or the whimpering of the freshman on the bed. The farmer heard it and went inside.

The liquor and exercise had made Ramsay warm. He had thrown off the blankets and lay half naked with his hands clasped across his eyes. Drops of sweat were running off his palpitating chest. Hill looked at his prettily developed arms and at the slender, well-turned wrist and at the tough little hands, which, Hill decided, had never done much farm work. Then because he liked what he saw, he laughed.

The light weight uncovered one eye and then covered it again.

"There, there," said the farmer, patting the black curly hair, which looked "pretty" against the white pillow. "I wouldn't take on so, little one, we'll get some of those canes yet."

Brandy and defeat had made Ramsay cross. He said: "Oh, go to the devil, won't you please?"

"All right," replied the big fellow. "Only you'll catch cold that way. Let me fix them." He carefully tucked the blankets around his classmate, who said, "That's so. Much obliged." Hill smiled at his uncomfortable tone.

When, after seven hard-fought rounds, Murray, the middle weight, was brought up breathless and caneless, there was great discouragement in the freshman camp. The middle weight was the one above all others upon whom they had relied to defend the honor of the class. Murray, the long-winded, himself had felt confident of winning; and probably he would have by sheer endurance had not the sophomore taken him unawares by a very easy finger trick as they lay together on the ground resting.

But it was all over now, and the middle weight was stretched out on the bed beside Ramsay. He had not, however, fainted, and he was sullenly chewing a piece of gum he had had in his mouth during the struggle. He looked unconcerned. He made no excuses to those who told what a nervy fight he had made.

All the week previous the betting on the heavy weight had been two to one on the sophomore. But now three seniors from the enemy's camp swaggered into the room shouting, "Here's four to one on Parker. Who wants it? Why don't you back your man?" They smiled at the junior coaches. "Drake don't want any of it," said another, in a dry tone; "he knows Parker too well."

Drake was the man who met Parker, unsuccessfully, the year before. "Wait a moment," he said. His sporting blood was stirred. "I'll take all you have, at four to one. Charlie, will you hold it, please?"

All of this must have been soothing to the nerves of the freshman heavy weight who was taking off his clothes for a final rub and trying not to hear the class cheers outside.

"Now then," said Montie Cunningham, slamming the door as the seniors hurried down the stairs, "this thing's got to stop right *here*." He brought a baseball bat down on the table so hard that every one stopped talking and looked up. "You've simply got to win that cane. If those dash sophomores win all three they'll crow over you for the rest of their course. They are arrogant enough already, dash them. And you fellows will be disgraced forever, and your class will be handed down in history as no good. People will refer to you as a class who lost all three canes. This is a crisis in your history. You made a good showing in the rush, but you were badly defeated in the baseball series. This is the third test. This decides it. Win this cane and you are all right. One out of three is a defeat, but not a disgrace, because you are only freshmen. But *none* out of three *is. You've got to win this cane!*"

No one uttered a sound for a moment. Farmer Hill did not laugh.

"Come here, Bushforth," said Drake, in a low, solemn voice; "I'll rub you myself."

The heavy weight was beautifully built and exceedingly quick for his size. He came to college with a good prep-school record of centre rush. But there was something disappointing about him, and you felt it every time you saw him move. You know the kind. One of those fellows who are splendid to look at in a football suit, and who will always put up a fair game on the scrub, but who are never going to make the 'Varsity.

Just now he was biting his lip and looking down at his own good legs. When he raised his glance he found Hill standing with arms akimbo, gazing at him with an earnest expression.

Bushforth smiled good-humoredly to show how cool he was.

"Think you can take that cane?" Hill asked with a grin.

"I really don't know, Hill," answered the beautifully built man.

"Do you think you can take it?" repeated the other.

"Well, Hill, Parker will have to work for it," said the heavy weight, indulgently. "Why? Would you like to take my place? I'd be glad to resign in your favor."

"All right," said Hill, simply. He began pulling up his sweater.

"Go on and sit down and stop your nonsense." It was hard to stand horse-play at such a moment, when your whole class was cheering for you outside.

"I ain't fooling," said the big farmer, with his arms still in the sweater, his head and body out.

"Hurry, Bush," said one of the juniors at the window. "The sophs have yelled across at me that they are ready."

"All right," said Bushforth, lacing his Jersey as he started for the door. He forgot to answer the other freshman.

"Wait a minute," said the big, cheerful voice of the farmer, "I think I'll go down this time."

"Oh, cork up, you big cow!" said Drake.

Hill corked up and then pushed Bushforth out of the way and started for the door.

"Will you please go back where you belong and sit down?" said Drake, impressively.

It failed to impress Hill. "Well, you see, it's this way," he began pleasantly, "he can't take that cane, I'm afraid. I can, though. I've got my blood up." He began contracting his biceps playfully. "Isn't it time to——"

"Freshman," interrupted Drake, with irony, "we have chosen the heavy weight representative of your class, and we are of the opinion that we know about as much of this business as you do. I never heard of such foolishness. Go sit down, and shut your big face. Your services will not be required unless Billy is laid off before he reaches the foot of the entry stairs. Come on, Billy."

"Then," Hill answered, smilingly, "I'll have to lay him off." He suddenly grabbed his big classmate by the shoulders, jerked him back into his arms, grasped him like a bag of flour, and hoisted him on his shoulders as if he had been one. "Now you lie down there, and be a good boy." He dropped Bushforth, but not roughly, in the corner behind the door, and then looked beamingly about at the others as though he had performed quite a feat. And so he had. Bushforth weighed one hundred and eighty-nine, stripped.

Outside the crowd was yelling concertedly in quick, jerky notes, "Shake it up! Shake it up! Shake it up!" and the sophomores were singing "Where, oh, where are the verdant freshmen?" etc., "Lost now in the green, green soup." But upstairs everyone was so tense and so excited that nothing was heard but the angry words of the coachers addressed to Hill, who was grinning.

Bushforth arose from the floor slowly.

"Shake it up, Billy," cried Drake, exasperated; "do you want to lose your cane by default?"

"Say," replied Bushforth, soberly, "do you suppose there's anything the matter with this hand?—Ugh! Great Scott! don't squeeze it."

Hill had not thrown him violently, but Bushforth, in throwing out his arms to stop himself, had struck his left hand against the wooden door-guard a few inches above the floor behind the door, and all his weight was upon it. The junior coach shut his eyes, dropped into Hill's big chair, and let his arms fall down to his sides. Everyone looked at him. "That settles it," he gasped. "Billy's hand is sprained. Let's give up the cane by default and——"

"Is it sprained?" interrupted Hill, removing his smile suddenly. "I'm sorry I hurt his hand. I did not intend that—Mr. Bushforth, I beg your pardon. I just wanted to show these fellows how strong I was. I didn't think I had a fair trial at spreeing. And now, Drake, don't you think we had better go down? They are clamoring down there. Are you coming?"

His tones were very deliberate and his manner so calm in contrast to the boiling condition of the others, that everyone seemed stunned for a moment. They only looked at one another.

"Shake it up! Shake it up! Shake it up!" came from the crowd below, and just then two representatives from the sophomores came running up the stairs, shouting, "Say, if you fellows don't wish to lose this by default come right now. Everyone's tired of waiting."

"Don't get excited," Drake shouted back. "Bushforth met with an accident and the sub is going to take his place. Come on, Hill." It was the only thing to do.

Hill saw the eyes of the two seniors brighten at the news, and heard his own classmates in the room cursing him. He said to himself, "Now then, I guess I've got to do something this evening," and followed Drake down the stairs.

"You're stronger than he is. He's all bluff. You'll do him dead easily," the two coachers were saying as heartily as they could. Hill did not reply. They crossed the light from the entry door. A strong cheer went up for Bushforth. Hill laughed. The coachers shivered.

Before they had pushed their way through the crowd to the ring, word went around that at the last moment Bushforth was laid off, and that a big sub named Hill had taken his place. Few had ever heard the name. The freshmen groaned; Hill heard it.

As they emerged into the ring, he heard a strange voice saying, "Why, he's that great big awkward chap the sophs guy so much, don't you remember?" Again Hill laughed.

"That's all right," whispered one of the juniors as he helped him off with his sweater. "You go in and win this cane, and your class will give you anything you want. Keep cool now, and remember what you have learned."

The farmer's big deformity-like shoulders looked more huge than ever in the thin, white jersey as he now straightened up in the moonlight.

"'Ray! 'Ray! 'Ray! Tiger, Siss, Boom, Ah! Hill." It rang out sharply on the frosty air. Then came a long cheer and then more short ones, with "Hill" on the end of them.

There is a peculiar thrill at the sound of one's own name shouted by a hundred voices on the end of a cheer. Hill felt it. He liked the feeling. "Now that means me," he said to himself, and he recalled what Drake had said to the middle weight: "Now remember, your whole class is watching you." It was in that moment that Hill caught class spirit.

The heavy weight spree was usually the shortest and most exciting contest of the evening. Everyone eagerly pressed forward on the wet grass.

The sophomores were barking and guying and quacking exultingly. The freshmen were cheering hard.

"Get ready, boys," said Jim, the athletic trainer, acting as referee. He held out the stick.

The sophomore ran out briskly. Hill spat on his hands and took his time about it. They grasped the cane. "Down in front, *please!*" a voice pleaded. The cheering had ceased as suddenly as you turn off the gas.

Hill was cool. He looked about at the theatre of faces on all sides. Just over the sophomore's shoulder, down on the ground with moonlight on his face, he spied an important-looking senior, with glasses, who on the campus had always seemed oblivious to the existence of freshmen. He was rocking back and forth and chewing a cold cigar to bits.

"Are you ready, Hill?"

The freshman spread his legs apart and said, "Yep."

"Ready, Parker?"

"Yes."

A ghastly silent second. "Spree!"

As the referee spoke the word, Hill felt the sophomore drop. He knew what was coming. Over his opponent's head he went sprawling on the grass, as he expected. But just then, in some manner, quick as a flash, Parker doubled and threw both legs in between Hill's body and the cane, and began, with all his strength, to strain, and push, and wrench.

Hill had expected something, and thought he was guarding against it. But this was a new trick—a variation on the old one—which the sophomore had invented himself.

Now, if it had been an ordinary man, with ordinary Christian shoulders, the strain would have been too great, and the sophomore would have won the cane in ten seconds, as he counted on doing.

But you see Hill was somewhat deformed as to his shoulders. He grunted and clung on, and the sophomore's coachers were yelling fiendishly: "You've got him, Park! you've got him!"

The next instant, while the sophomore was trying to better his advantage, Hill quietly turned, slipped out of the perilous position, and drew himself up close to the sophomore's body. He lay there panting, while his coachers cried, joyfully: "Good one, Hill! good one!" and his classmates left off feeling sick at their stomachs, and began to cheer him by name. This he did not hear.

He had been taken by surprise at the fall, but now he was entirely alive to what he was about. Every nerve was at tension, each muscle set at hair-trigger. There was just one thing in all the world to him now, and that was the cane. And when, a moment later, Parker began a quick series of furious jerks, back and forth and sidewise, Hill said, half aloud: "No, you don't, old man," and smiled confidently to himself as he felt how firm the cane was in his hand.

The sophomore, on top, now tried working Hill's hands off with his fingers. But the freshman had lived on a farm all his life. Then he tried something with his legs. But Hill's big supports were as hard as the columns of Whig Hall, though not as symmetrical. Then, waiting awhile, he tried to surprise Hill with more quick, sharp wrenches. It was unsuccessful. He waited, and tried it again. Then time was called. The two class-cheers burst forth simultaneously.

The contestants were dragged to their respective corners, wrapped with blankets, and sponged with water.

During the interval, a buzz of voices began suddenly, as in a racing grand-stand after the winner has been announced. The college had expected an easy thing for Parker, the champion, and when they heard of Bushforth's absence, they were sure of it. Everyone was saying: "Who is this Hill? Hasn't he shoulders! Wasn't that a narrow hole he crawled out of?"

The coachers were whispering, "You're doing well, Hill. Stick to him, and you'll get him yet. You'll tire him out."

Two or three freshmen came into the ring and shook Hill's hand, saying, nervously, "Good boy, Hill, good one." He was already a distinguished man, having held the cane for a round against Parker. But Hill only grinned and had his own opinion. The honor of the class depended upon him. He thought he was going to win the cane.

When the referee called them up, one of the sophomore's coaches called out, in an easy tone, "Remember, now," and Parker replied, in a cool way, "Very well." The silence was worse than ever. People felt that this would be the last round.

The two spreers were the coolest on the campus. But they also felt that this would settle it, and as they grasped the cane each looked the other over and then gazed straight into his enemy's eye. Very much, no doubt, as knights of old used to size each other up before they fell to cutting each other to bits, of a quiet afternoon by the sea-side.

Hill did not like Parker, nor would he have fancied him even if the sophomore had not been a brutal and unreasonable hazer. However, he appreciated his athletic abilities, and even in the tense moment of waiting for the referee's word, he could not help admiring the way his opponent's neck fitted his body, and the clean cut of his limbs, which Hill himself so lacked.

The sophomore looked him back in the eyes, and said, sneeringly, "You damned freshman!" which was entirely uncalled for.

When the word was given both kept their feet for a few minutes. They held their arms down stiff, keeping the cane close to their bodies in order to prevent the other from jumping in between. Neither seemed inclined to begin the attack, and they danced cautiously about the circle with their faces close together. There was something impressive in the sight of these two, pounding about in the moonlight. They were so ponderous, and it all seemed to mean so much. Parker tried the right hip throw.

He was partially successful. They were both on the ground now, and the timer snapped his stop watch. Time is not counted when the men are erect.

The sophomore was on top again. Again he tried his jerking manœuvres, and again Hill smiled to himself and thought, "I guess not."

He lay perfectly still on the wet grass, as if comfortable and quite content to remain there. He heard a voice from the crowd say, "Spread out, you coachers. Give us a show." He could feel the sophomore's breath on his neck and the beating of the heart against his back. He felt the cool wet grass on his cheek flattened against it, and he became aware that his nose was bleeding, and then said to himself, "Oh, yes; I must have bumped that on Parker's elbow when we came down."

Now, up to this point, the freshman had been on the defensive entirely, and he had been so successful that one of the coachers began giving the signals to begin a little offensive work. "No, no, Hammie," cried Drake. "Let good enough alone."

Hill had regained his wind by this time. "Please don't bother me," he said, in a muffled tone. "I'm doing this thing. I'll get this cane in a minute." This was loud enough for some of those in the crowd to hear. Somehow it sounded horrible.

And it seemed to enrage Parker. He began a furious onslaught, as if he were tired of playing with a freshman so long and meant to end the thing right there.

He wrenched and jerked this way, he tugged and pulled that way, he turned over and then back, he tried all the manœuvres he knew, and took desperate chances, which the freshman was too slow to take advantage of. Twice the sophomore seemed to have the cane, and the freshman still held on. It was a battle of giants, and those that were there will never forget it.

And while they struggled, now one on top and now the other, they rolled over to the extreme lower part of the circle toward the path leading to the railway station. That part of the audience fell back. The ring broke. Some closed in around them.

Then, while the referee was shouting, "Get back! Get back!" the freshman was suddenly seen to rise on his knees yelling shrilly, like a wild beast in pain. "You would bite me, would you, you——." He sprang to his feet. The blood from his nose was smeared all over his face. A furious wrench jerked Parker from the ground. With what was extraordinary power Hill whirled him; part of the way the feet dragged, though some like to tell that the whole of Parker was clean in the air all the way round; he whirled him about, as you would whirl a pillow with both arms; then, suddenly reversing all his big weight and simultaneously twisting the hickory, he snapped the sophomore off in the air and lifted the cane high and dry above his head. "The freshman has it," shrieked a shrill voice.

He felt himself grabbed, he heard many noises, he went up, up in the air, and then he forgot.

The big leather chair was the first thing he saw, and he knew he was in the Witherspoon room again. Then he heard many voices talking at once. He remembered now that he had been hearing them for ages. They echoed inside his head some place.

"Are you all right now?"

He raised his lids a little higher and there was Drake bending over him as tenderly as a mother.

"I think you ought to know, you great big awkward old farmer, that you saved the day for us." Drake looked as delighted as if he had done it himself.

"I've seen a good many sprees," said another voice near his head, which Hill had never heard before, "but that was the finest thing I ever saw; and I'm blame glad you did him, though I *am* a senior and lost twenty-five bats on it." Hill moved his head and saw the important-looking senior with glasses.

The farmer now laughed his hideous laugh. That showed he was all right.

One of the sophomore coachers approached the bed, and after looking up and down Hill's bulk a moment, said: "The trouble with you, you big freshman, is that you don't know when you're beaten. My man had that cane twice, but you wouldn't let go."

"Well, that's Princeton spirit, isn't it?" remarked the 'Varsity Captain, who had something to say to Hill later on.

Ramsay, the light weight, came running up the entry three steps at a time. He had been leading cheers for Hill out-doors and now he began hugging him. "Oh, farmer, you're a dandy. Give me your hand."

But when the farmer raised his hand he found the cane was still in it. "Here, little one, you can have this. I've had my fun out of it." This showed how green he was.

"No," said Ramsay; "you're to keep that forever. What did you win it for, anyway?"

As a matter of fact winning the spree meant much more to the big placid farmer than a hickory cane to hang with ribbons over his mantelpiece, and more than a bit of fame in another kind of athletics, too. Much more. As we all know now.

THE MADNESS OF POLER STACY

In freshman year they say, "Are you ready to feed your face?" instead of "Are you going to dinner?" and at the eating clubs they call the milk-pitcher the "cow," and shout "Butter me, please," when they wish the butter handed to them. All their desires and opinions they express in variously bold and vulgar metaphors, which are witty. This is because there is no one to tell them they must not. The boy is a college man now. He is free from the restraint of home or school or both, and he doesn't know quite what to do with his liberty.

Like a young town horse turned loose for the first time in the open green of the country, he sometimes loses his head and frisks and snorts and kicks up his heels to an unbecoming degree. This is a way of saying that every once in a while some little boy (the strictly reared kind, usually), in his eagerness to show his fellows how reckless and devilish he is, goes so far that he never comes quite back. Others dissipate merely to the extent of cutting chapel twice in succession or pretending that they have not poled all night for an examination. In still others it breaks out in a different form, and they persuade themselves that they are naughty cynics or bold, bad agnostics. But that will do for that.

The point is this: Sooner or later, in some form or another, this spirit is bound to get hold of every young man who is worthy of the name, and, like measles or calf-love, it is better to have it sooner. In the very young it is interesting. After that it is not. And the older one is when it comes, the more he reminds the onlookers of the frolicksome antics of some ancient, misguided cow, or of a kittenish summer girl, aged twenty-eight. When seen in a poler it is pathetic.

At his first eating club in freshman year, H. Stacy felt himself snubbed from the start; and when the crowd, which was not slow, became well enough acquainted with one another and with the glorious freedom of college life to pour syrup down their neighbors' backs and to hurl fried eggs and coarse jokes about the table, little Stacy, although he always said, "That was a pretty good shot," and wiped the potato from his ear with a noisy laugh, saw that he was not in his own element, which he should have seen a month before, and got out.

He joined a club of a very different sort of freshmen, who were too busy speculating upon their chances at the approaching Divisional Examinations to invent names for tough beefsteak, or learn what was going on in Trenton at the theatres and other places.

This was his element. He drew in long, full breaths of freedom and sunshine, and told himself that now he knew what was meant by the Joy of College Life.

Here he settled down to the methodical poler habits he was intended for, and when the next catalogue was issued his mother and sister pointed out to the minister's wife the name of "Horatio B. Stacy, New Jersey," in the small group of names called "First Group," and said, "We knew he would do it." In his sophomore year he did it again and won a prize or two besides and became a minor light in the Cliosophic Society, and by this time he held in that Hall an office, the name of which was a secret, and could not be divulged even to his sister Fannie. He studied for high marks and was called a "greasy poler." But he got the high marks.

You must not think he had no friends. He made some firm ones. About these he could write home to his sister Fannie, telling what magnificent characters some of them were. Often of a Saturday night, if he had no essays to write or debates to prepare, he slipped off his eye-shades and pattered across the campus to his friends' rooms and knocked gently and said, "How do?" and conversed for an hour on the difficulty of taking notes when your neighbor is borrowing your knife, or about the elective courses for the next term. And down at the club they had great horse calling each other "Blamed Neo-Platonists" and "Doggoned Transcendentalists." Nor was it all shop. One of them thought himself in love. It was Stacy that used to wink at the others and bob his head and say, "I know some one who got a letter to-day." They had great fun at the club.

By reason of his freshman year's disgust he remained innocent, which was right, and ignorant, which was wrong, of much that he might have experienced, and he bade fair to graduate a typical poler with a bad breath and an eye on Commencement stage and special honors. Sometimes, to be sure, dark questions arose in his mind, strange, shameful yearnings that caused him to read whole pages without taking in a word of it. But then, all polers have wild moments when they feel that they would rather play on the team than win the Stinnecke Scholarship, so Stacy should not have been distressed.

But sometimes it seemed to him that even those classmates whom he knew only slightly and did not understand at all, those fellows who seemed to do nothing but loaf about the campus all day and sing and shout at night, while he was running his hands through his hair and his eyes through Kant's "Critique of Pure Reason," they, it seemed to him, were getting a poetry out of college life that he was missing. "But never mind," he would say to himself. "They will regret it some day. They will wish they had done as I am doing, instead of wasting golden opportunities which come but once and which glide by like ships upon the sea of life." Then he would pull his hair and start at the top of the page again. It is better to have First Group than the Glee Club.

But there were some fellows who could do both. Some fellows stood high in the class and were in with everybody besides. Why could not he be like that? This question came to him quite suddenly in junior year, and he tipped his head to one side and began to think about it. He kept on thinking.

He was still thinking about it one Sunday afternoon in chapel when big Jack Stehman, the tackle, came stalking down the aisles and threw himself down beside Stacy, and the oak creaked. He was fresh and clean and rosy from a long 'cross country tramp, and he said, "Hello, Stace," in a hearty whisper. It was not from policy like the smiling hello of a man a few pews in front, but because he felt like it. Stacy enjoyed being saluted in that way, and if the big fellow grabbed and pinched his thin leg he would beam for the rest of the hour, even though he found a blue spot there at night when he undressed in Edwards Hall.

It was because of his way of saying hello, as much as his great football record, that Stehman was one of the most popular men in college, and nobody worshipped him more than did Stacy, not even the freshman who gazed across the pews and wondered what it would be like to be on familiar terms with a man of that sort. Stacy had at one time feared that there was something sinful in his own admiration; Stehman was a fourth-group man.

He was thinking that his big class-mate looked just as strong and clean and good as during the season. Just then Timberly, in the pew behind, lay hold of Stehman's hair, drew his head back against the rail, and then rubbed his own vigorously against Stehman's. "Little Jackie's had his long locks cut, hasn't he?" he said. His teeth were gritted and there was a sweet caress in his Southern voice, for he loved his good pal Jack Stehman, though he would have called you profane things if you had accused him of it. Stehman smiled, and said, "Let go, Timber, you ass, the organ has stopped."

Little Stacy, watching this out of the corner of his glasses, said, solemnly, "I'd give my first group for that," and then bowed his head in prayer. He thought about it all through the service instead of listening as he should have done to a returned missionary who told how many widows there were in India under thirteen years of age, and other interesting things.

The next day, when he walked with Stehman from a lecture by the Dean on Robert Southey, he tried to catch his friend's tone of hello. Jack said it to about fifty men between Dickinson Hall and Reunion, and it sounded as though he were glad to see everyone of them, and he was. Stacy liked to be seen with the big fellow. But he did not blush and keep silent as in sophomore year when he was first permitted to walk with him. He tried to show everyone that he was used to it.

This time something happened. When they reached the place where the stone walks meet, in front of South Reunion, Stehman put a big hand on his shoulder, and said, "Stace, will you dine with me this evening?—Oh, yes, you can. I have an engagement in Dougal's room now. I'll yell for you on the way to the club. So long." Stacy opened his mouth and gazed after him until out of sight. Then he shut it and started for his room. This was unexpected.

He had often thought about these large swell clubs with their elective membership, and he had walked by the houses when the members were lounging out in front. He had heard snatches of songs and the click of billiard-balls from within, and he wondered what they did and said and how it looked inside. And now he was going to see one of them, the one he admired the most of all.

At his own little eating club, he and the others said that many of the club men were snobs, and declared that they would have nothing to do with them. He wondered if his friends envied them in secret, as he did. At any rate he would not dread answering them the next morning when they asked, "Where were you for dinner?"

When he reached his room he changed his necktie for a more becoming one. At least he thought it was. And he put on his new, heavy, tan shoes, like those Stehman and so many fellows wore. He would show them that he knew things. Then he sat down and wrote to his sister Fannie about it, as he did once before with a trembling hand, when he won that essay prize in Hall and came late to dinner in consequence, and all the fellows cried, "Yea-a, Stacy, Sophomore essay prize!" He had pointed out that club to Fannie when she and his mother came over at Commencement, and he had told her that Stehman was in that one. She knew who Stehman was.

Stacy little imagined that he was of so much consequence, but Stehman, the tackle, had been talking about him on Sunday evening by the club fireplace. Two of the fellows who were younger than juniors ought to be had smiled at what he said.

To them Jack turned with some heat, and observed, "You fellows make me tired. You aren't under-class men now; you're old enough to know better than to size up people by under-class man standards. Just because Stacy has not learned to swear or smoke, and because he worries and fusses and gets pale over what he came to college for, you think you have a right to laugh at him. I respect him, and I wish to the deuce I was more like him. Little

Stacy is all right. And he'll be in it all right some of these days, and he'll do a great deal more good in the world than most of us."

This was the longest speech Jack Stehman had ever made, and he was duly applauded and guyed for it. But he was serious. He had a Sunday night sour on. It was junior year for Stehman also, and he too had been coming to some conclusions about his college course. But of a different kind.

It was nearly half after six when Stacy heard his friend's big voice echo across the campus. As he pattered down the stairs in his stiff, new Bluchers, he could not help wishing that Stehman had come a little earlier. Not that he was hungry, but the campus would then have been more crowded, while Stehman called, "Hello, Ray Stace."

As they passed under the lamp-post and Jack said "Hello" to somebody going in the other direction, Stacy remembered how that once he would not have believed that he should ever be walking as he was now with Stehman's big, strong arm upon his shoulder, the same arm that had brought down many a canvas jacket. But that was long ago.

When they reached the club, Stehman kicked the mud from his big, heavy shoes on the porch steps, and Stacy did the same for his bright new little ones. The door flew open and the brightly lighted interior of the club was before them. Stacy caught a glimpse of an open fire and deep, comfortable places to lounge in beside it, and some etchings on the wall. He heard knives and forks and many voices, all going at once, and laughter and exclamations. He spied a waiter hurrying in with a tray full of dishes. A little nigger boy, with innumerable buttons on his jacket, began to help him off with his overcoat, and just then he heard one voice exclaim emphatically, "Doc., I say they can't do it," and he wondered what it was and who could not do it.

Stehman said, "Come over here a moment—no, this way."

"Oh, this way?" said Stacy. He was led to a large open book with names written on it.

"Will you give us your distinguished signature?" said Stehman, dipping the pen in ink and handing it to him.

"Where shall I write—oh, yes, of course." Stacy wondered how many people would read Horatio B. Stacy, introduced by John Carter Stehman.

Though he had made up his mind to have confidence he felt a little flustered. Perhaps the voices of many diners and the sight of many rooms and various passage-ways and the negro buttons were a little too much for him. Besides his glasses were blurred at coming in from the cold and that always rattled him.

Possibly his host noticed this, for he said, "Boo, I'm cold. Let's warm up before grubbing," and led him to the fire and pushed him into a chair big enough to hold two Horatio B. Stacys.

He was perspiring now, but he held out his hand to the cheerful blaze as if to get all he could of it. He looked at the andirons and the crackling wood and glanced up at the etchings. He thought, "It must be very fine to have all this every day."

"Well, do you feel as though you could eat something?" Stehman lifted him by the coat-collar.

Stacy made answer, in a familiar tone, "I'm ready any time you are, Jack," and then to himself, "Keep cool now."

Stehman, with his hands in his pockets, led the way with his slouching football walk which the freshmen studied on the way to recitations. Stacy followed. He slouched pretty well, but his pockets were at the very top of his trousers, so that his little coat turned up behind.

They entered the bright, noisy dining-room. "Jack, why so late?" some one was calling out, when suddenly there came, "Hello, Stace." "Hello, Kay." "Hello there, Stace." "How do do, Stace." Most all of them seemed glad to see him, and he was quite overcome with answering them all. Jack showed him where to sit.

After the waiter had pushed the chair under him and he had unfolded the napkin there came in a solemn voice from the end of the table, "Horatio, how do you do this evening?"

"Why, Lint, old man, how are you?" he returned quickly in a strong tone. Then he smiled a little because Linton might be guying him. But he was not.

It seemed that many eyes were upon him and he felt embarrassed and strangely lonely because his host had turned to speak about something to someone on the other side. So he gave his glasses an unnecessary rub and took three sips of water in quick succession.

The waiter placed the soup before him, and while he was occupied with it he had time to gather himself together. Some of the fellows, he noticed over his glasses, leaned over or else slipped way down in their chairs in the same purposely reckless manner of under-classmen days. But he held his little shoulders back and used his spoon very daintily. He would show them that he had good table manners.

Stehman now began to chat with him in his easy familiar way. But the big fellow's manner always seemed to indicate that he was mindful of how much higher was Stacy's class rank than his own.

He was more at ease now, only whenever the conversation flagged he could never think up anything to renew it with. He suspected that he was blushing, and there really was no reason for blushing. These were all his own dear classmates, some of whom he knew quite well, and they all seemed kindly disposed toward him and included him in their general remarks and even addressed him sometimes in particular. He made up his mind that he must say something to Dougal Davis across the table.

He took a drink of water and wiped his lips and cleared his throat and spoke. "Dougal, have you poled up Billy's history for the written recitation?" Which was the very sort of thing he meant to avoid. But it was too late now.

"No, but I expect to put a wet towel around my head and hit it up until three o'clock to-night," Dougal answered, sincerely.

And Stacy thought he was joking. He therefore laughed, saying, "Like fun you are."

He never could tell when some of these fellows were in earnest, and Dougal Davis was something awful to him anyway because he stood higher in the class than Stacy himself, and yet had time to be mixed up with half a dozen outside interests of college life and did a comfortable amount of loafing besides.

"I suppose you have it all down fine, Stace?" asked Timberly, agreeably, "and will pound out a first group as usual."

"Naw," boldly replied Stacy, "I've barely looked at it. Don't intend to bother with it." That was the way to talk.

But it was all wasted, for just then Lamason came in with a suit-case in his hand and his town clothes on, and everybody was crying "Yea-a" in loud, shrill tones, and some one began singing "Oh, to-day is the day that he comes from the city," and all joined in, even little Stacy, though he did not know the words and blushed and closed his mouth again when any one looked in his direction.

Meanwhile Lamason, without smiling, or seeming to be aware of the noise, said, "Bring me some dinner, Henry, please," and taking a *Princetonian* from his pocket began to read an editorial on the lack of lamp-posts on the south campus, and paid no more attention to the remarks about his good-looking clothes than to Timberly, who was painstakingly mussing up his nicely brushed hair. It impressed Stacy. Except that they no longer considered it funny to throw things or to be profane without necessity, the fellows seemed to be as free and jolly as in under-classmen days. He had supposed that there would be some dignity about a great fine elective club with white curtains at the window and a board of governors.

While beginning upon his roast beef the waiter placed a small, narrow glass by his plate. He heard the "pop" of a drawn cork behind him. He had understood that the club constitution forbade alcoholic beverages. The waiter was filling his glass. He heard something hiss and sizzle, but he did not like to look because it would be so obvious. This would be a good opportunity to show these fellows that he was not such a shark as they supposed. Still, after keeping out of temptation so many years, he did not like the idea of running the risk of becoming a drunkard now. But, perhaps, it would not be wrong to taste a little of it.

"Are you fond of Apollinaris, Ray?" asked Stehman, emptying his glass at a gulp. "I'm a disgusting guzzler of it."

"Oh, yes, I'm—I like it very much," said Stacy. Stehman asked him to have another piece of roast just to keep him company, and without giving time for answer, Stacy heard him say, "Two second, Henry—rare." Jack made him drink another bottle of Apollinaris, too, though it pricked his tongue, and he said he did not want it, and he felt that he was imposing upon his friend when he saw him write out another voucher for the amount.

Most of the table had finished by this time. They were smoking with their coffee. Those who could afford it were smoking cigars and those who had used up their credit with the Cigar Committee were solacing themselves with pipes. Some there were who did not smoke at all.

"Our crowd," Jack explained, "makes it a matter of principle never to leave the table for a half hour or so. It's good for the digestion."

Three or four of the fellows were leaning back with their heads on the backs of chairs or on one another's shoulders. One was slouching with his elbow on the table and with his other hand he played with the salt-cellars. And some looked perfectly contented and happy, and some looked grave or sour, and all were beautifully and completely indolent, and everything seemed comfortable and happy and Bohemian to Stacy, and he thought it fine to eat his dessert with the smoke floating about it.

Dougal Davis opposite was blowing fat, well-formed rings aimed at the top of Stacy's Apollinaris bottle, while Linton, without looking up, was informing him, in picturesque, though hardly complimentary language, that he had a mouth splendidly adapted to ring-blowing. Davis kept on sending rings across the table, and paid no attention. Stacy wondered whether they were on bad terms with one another. Perhaps it was rude in him to listen. They seemed so much in earnest.

It was difficult to understand these fellows. Some of them he knew to be as hard students as himself, and yet they seemed to be as much in with the crowd as the others. Someone would say something in a most impressive, sober way, and nobody seemed to notice it, or else everyone laughed. Of course he knew that what they were saying during dinner about their extreme poverty was meant humorously, even by those of the fellows who tutored or wrote for the papers to help themselves along. But what troubled him was that he could not catch the drift and join in and be like the rest of them. Once, when everybody laughed heartily, and Pope bowed his head and said, "I acknowledge that I am sat upon," Stacy laughed, too, and said "Pretty good," though he did not know what it was, and hoped that no one knew he was bluffing.

From another part of the house came the pounding of billiard-cues and a few emphatic remarks, varied at intervals with a yell or a loud laugh. In another room three or four voices were singing, perhaps unconsciously, and the strong final notes reached the dining-room. Upstairs someone was exclaiming, "I had next on that!" From the lounging room came the notes of a piano, and Stacy said, "That 'Pilgrim's Chorus' is a beautiful thing, isn't it, Jack?" for Stacy knew.

He had enjoyed his dinner, and was perfectly self-possessed. He could look about the room at everyone without flinching. Henry brought the coffee in very pretty cups, with the club design on them. The buttons came in at Stehman's ringing. "Jackson, get me a —— Ray, you don't smoke, do you?"

"Oh, yes, I do," Stacy replied.

"Oh, I beg your pardon—bring some Perfectos, Jackson—please pardon me, I forgot entirely that you smoked. I must have mixed you up with someone else. I thought sure you did not smoke."

He seemed so cut up about it and his voice so pathetically apologetic that Stacy felt sorry for him, and had to say, "That's all right, Jack. You see I have just begun. That is, I haven't been smoking very long, you know, on account of my eyes." But he hoped the others did not hear.

"Will you have a cigarette first?" Stehman asked.

"No, I prefer a cigar," said Stacy, in a fine, deep voice. Stehman lighted a cigarette.

Horatio had never smoked but one cigar before, and he was not certain about how much of the end to bite off. But it seemed to draw all right when the buttons held a match for him. It did not make him feel the least bit sick. He thought he held it between his first and second fingers rather well.

His host began to talk about the Dean's English again, and Stacy changed the subject. Of course Jack meant it out of consideration for him, but Stacy could talk about other things than his studies. Presently Jack began again. "What collateral reading are you doing in the Public Law course, Ray—— What's that you're saying, Timber?"

"Oh, nothing," said Timberly, smiling satirically. "We are just amused a little bit at your posing as a heavy poler. That's all."

But Jack only frowned, and turned again to Stacy, who knew the others were paying attention, and so made answer, "Don't intend to read anything. I've quit taking notes on the lectures, too. A syllabus at the end of the term will have to do me." That ought to show them.

Nobody said anything for a moment, and when he looked up he could not tell from their faces what they thought of his remark, though Linton seemed to wear a quizzical smile. But then that fellow always seemed to be sneering or else looking oblivious.

Then Smith, who was a track athlete, went on with his conversation with Pope. He was venturing the opinion that Princeton's prospects for the spring were poor. He was a young man who thought he had a dignity, and he liked to have people pay attention to what he said. He had reason to suppose that his opinions on athletics amounted to something. So he was rather astonished, as were Stehman and the rest of the table, when Stacy's high voice burst in with, "No, now, you don't mean it, Smithie. You are joking, aren't you?" There was no reason why he should not be familiar and play horse like the rest.

At first there was such a pause that he felt himself blush, and he feared he had offended Smith, who had stopped talking and was blushing a little, too. Then suddenly Timberly burst out with a snorting laugh, and then Davis and then the whole crowd, even Linton, and Stacy himself, because he had made such a hit, laughed modestly, though still blushing, at which they all laughed still more. He did not know it was so funny as all that. That was not half as witty as he could be, as he would show them.

But just then Stehman interrupted and claimed attention. "Timber," he called down the table, "I heard a new one to-day on Jimmie McCosh." Stehman then told a story about the Doctor's falling on the slippery stones on McCosh walk, and what he said when he could not get up. Like most imitations of dear old Jimmie's Scotch, Stehman's sounded like a poor Irish brogue. It was not a very good story, but the fellows imagined how it would sound if told well, and then laughed because it was good old Jack Stehman. Stacy thought he could do better than that.

Everything was quiet. Now was the time. He cleared his throat. "Say, fellows, this is the way the president talks in chapel." His voice was high and unnecessarily loud. He arose and took hold of the lapels of his little coat and raised his brows and compressed his lips and looked side wise through his glasses and repeated very quickly in a strange voice, "The seven Arabic numerals do not form a sufficient basis for crystallization about which the cardinal virtues may cluster." Then he promptly sat down and began to puff vigorously upon his big cigar.

The fellows smiled surprisedly and looked at each other. Then they laughed. They stopped a moment; then one by one they began to laugh again, as if the thing were growing on them. Finally they roared and kept on roaring.

At home they always applauded when he got that off, although his mother thought it wrong in him, but they did not pound on the table and scream and slap each other on the back, as these fellows were doing now. It must have been because this audience was more familiar with the original. But he hardly heard them.

"Say, fellows, I'll tell you the story of the little boy who stole the jam!" he exclaimed, excitedly. Before Stehman and one or two others of this same crowd he had tried once in freshman year to tell this same story, and failed for lack of courage. He was not the least bit frightened this time.

He leaned back in his chair and imitated the boy's voice and blew smoke between sentences and gesticulated with the cigar in his hand; and when he had finished everyone pounded and screamed and applauded as before, while he only shut his lips tight and tried to look serious, as all good *raconteurs* should. Would not this be fine to write to Fannie about?

"Good! Good!" they were shouting to him. "Give us another, Stace. You're a good one. Do the Dr. Patton act again. These fellows haven't seen it."

"No, we haven't seen it. Let her go."

Stacy raised his eyes from the table-cloth. Those of the juniors that had left and some of the seniors, hearing the racket, had come in to see what was up. The piano had ceased. Fellows were pushing into the room with cues in their hands and their coats off. Some of them were sitting on the table. Some had their arms about one another's shoulders. Leaning against the door-post, with a pipe in his mouth and a merry twinkle in his eye, stood a senior named Bangs, whom Stacy, in freshman year, feared more than anything on earth. He had never, until this moment, forgiven him.

Before Bangs and over half the active membership of the club did little Stacy, who used to cross the street to avoid being looked at, jump up on a chair and with greater gusto than ever, with his funny little mouth twisted up, with his voice strained to produce a peculiar resonance, repeat part of a sermon once preached by the president of the college. And when he had finished, his hearers were doubled up on the floor with laughter.

Throughout all this Stehman alone seemed unappreciative. He laughed in a nervous way. Once he said, "Let's go sit by the fire." Could it be possible that his good friend Jack, who was accustomed to being the most popular, was—no, he would not think that of him.

"Do something else," they were crying. "Go on. Go on. Please!"

If he wanted to he could double them up once more, this time with an imitation of Jimmie Johnson's stuttering, but he absolutely declined. He knew that brevity was the soul of wit. "Stacy, you ought to go on the stage!" one of the seniors exclaimed.

But he only answered, "Naw. That don't amount to anything. Shoot." And then they all began laughing once more at the mere remembrance of it.

Jack arose to go. Stacy picked up the huge cigar, which had gone out, and jamming it firmly between his teeth, strode after his host. He walked past the fellows, who were still laughing, as modestly and with as unconscious an expression as Jack Stehman himself wore on the football field when running back to his place after making a touch-down and the crowd was cheering.

In the hall he said, "I think I'll have to go now, Jack." His voice was joyously nervous. He could not hold in much longer.

"Must you go, Ray?"

"Yes. I must finish a letter. Good-night, Jack, old man. I've had a bully time."

The buttons was helping him on with his coat, and he repeated, "Good-night, Jack, old man. I've had a bully time." His voice nearly broke.

Then the door closed, and Stehman, who was angry, turned toward the convulsing crowd by the fire and said, in a calm voice, "I greatly admire what you fellows have done this evening. You are indeed typical Princeton men. Oh, you have the true spirit."

"Fine poler, your quiet, inoffensive, young friend," some one rejoined with a chuckle.

"Not ashamed—as you were reminding us the other night—not ashamed of being a poler either," said the fellow Stehman had jumped on for being a kid.

"Wow!" cried Bangs, with a groan of laughter. "I haven't had so much horse since sophomore year."

Then Linton spoke. "Jackie, dear, don't look that way. It's not nice. And do not chew a rag because your little poler did not develop as you wanted him to. You must learn to part with your ideals———"

"And, Jack, you must admit," interrupted Davis, "that it was absurdly comical. It was mean to laugh, but how could we help it? His standing up there and kicking up his poler antics, like an old cow, and thinking all the time that he was———"

The rest was cut short by Stehman's bringing his big fist down upon a table by the window. "But, Dougal," he thundered, "that doesn't make any difference. He was my guest. Because he tried to bring himself down to our tone you fellows let him make a fool of himself, and sat there and laughed at him, like a set of snobs. Jackson, get my coat."

"You needn't talk so loud," growled a sarcastic-faced post-graduate. "The people across the street don't care to hear about it."

"Don't go away with your back up, Jack," Linton shouted after him good-naturedly. "And you need not worry about little Stacy. The best time he ever had in college was with us snobs here to-night, and he's probably chuckling to himself now on his way across the campus about the big tear he made."

But little Stacy was not doing anything of the sort. One of his new Blucher shoes had come untied when he had jumped up on the chair to do the president act, and he stopped to tie it by the light of the club window. And it was wide open.

THE HAZING OF VALLIANT

This story begins with a girl. She was small and had a nose that turned up and a quiet appreciation of the ridiculous. All summer long she sat on the sand without a veil and was nice to two little boys in clean duck trousers and buzz-saw hats which blew off sometimes.

One of these was eighteen years old and had a complexion that women envied and felt like kissing. He was small and dainty and smelt like good soap. His name was Valliant. The other was a little older, considerably bigger, and much more self-assertive. Except for his duck trousers he wore orange and black with his class numerals on everything. That might have made but little difference. But the girl decided that she would like it more if they would become angry for her sake, which they one day did.

After that whenever the little one was alone with her his voice was soft and his manner thoroughly abject. She liked this. She liked his sweet-and-cleanness also. The other, whose name was Buckley, had an untamed, defiant way of tossing his shoulders, like an unbroken stallion. She liked that still more. When she sat out dances with him, she put him where the arc-light on the veranda would play upon his eyes, which were good, and talked about the other boy's nice manners.

Best of all she liked to have both about her at once. The sophomore breathed lungfuls of cigarette smoke and told her how hard his class would haze the freshman in the fall, and how cold the canal was on a frosty night, while the sub-freshman only gazed out over the legs and arms splashing and gleaming in the surf, and tried to smile in a way to show Buckley that he was not taking offence. For what could a sub-freshman do?

Then the girl would poke the end of her red parasol in the sand and say: "I think it would be just too mean of you to haze Mr. Valliant. He is such a good friend of mine." This was because it is woman's nature to take the part of the weak and oppressed.

But one day the sophomore made a remark about "pretty pink-cheeked boys," which had been better left unsaid. Then arose the younger one and shaking impressively a slender, pink-nailed finger, he spoke. "You had better not try to haze me, Will Buckley. Do you hear what I say?" Which was the very worst thing he could have said. Besides it was decidedly fresh.

But he was very much in earnest and quite angry and his young voice broke in the middle. The sophomore laughed mirthfully and the girl became genuinely sorry for a moment, despite the humor of the situation; and as she watched his dainty legs retreating over the dunes toward the cottages it repented her of having stirred up enmity between the two, and she resolved from that day to make up for it. This she did by being always good to the little one in the presence of the big one, which seems short-sighted in her.

Thus did one small girl amuse herself throughout the week, and then, when Saturday evening came and the children were left to burn cigarettes by themselves, she entertained the men with it, who came down to spend Sunday. For her nose turned up and she was good at mimicry. She won't be mentioned again.

In the glorious old days of untrammelled class activity when everyone recognized that there were certain duties owed the freshman by the sophomore class, as Hall talk was due them from the upper-classmen (another good old custom now defunct), you had only casually to drop word to a freshman on the way to recitation to wait for you when night came, back of Witherspoon—as you would bid a classmate come to a spread in your room—and he would turn up promptly and smilingly, take his little dose meekly and cheerfully, and go to bed a better boy for it and brag about it every time he dined out in Christmas holidays. But all that is changed now.

Even in the days of which this is written, which were only comparatively modern times, one had to play a very careful game to do any hazing. The freshman was beginning to hesitate about putting out his light when you yelled up at him from the street. People were putting strange notions in his head. He was beginning to think he had a personality. They were telling him he had rights. The old glory had departed along with Rushes and Midnight Cane Sprees and Horn Sprees and Fresh Fires to make room for a University spirit and linen shirts. At the present rate of retrogression— mark the prediction—it will not be many years before the freshman will be allowed to wear the orange and black and the sophomore a silk hat! When that day comes, may it be that a certain Old Grad. will have attended his last reunion.

Twice had Buckley waited near the house where Valliant ate his dinner. But it's quite light after dinner in September. He had gone to the house where he roomed, and asked the landlady if any of the gentlemen wanted to join the Y. M. C. A. But that, like the *Nassau Lit.* and *Princetonian* subscription-list-game, had been played out; the door was closed in his face. Then for three successive nights he waited in an alley near by, and on the third night the freshman came. But with him an upper-classman friend.

Buckley said things and kept in the shadow. But the freshman had good eyes and said as he took out his keys, "Oh, is that you, Mr. Buckley? Why, how do you do? Aren't you coming up to see me?" That was horribly fresh.

"Not now," Buckley growled. "Which is your room?" Excusing himself from the upper-classman, who was enjoying all this, the freshman led Buckley into the alley-way, and pointed up at the wing of the house. It was a large one and many people lived in it. "That room up there next to the one with a light in it. See?" he said in polite, friendly tones. This was decidedly fresh.

Buckley said he would come up later on in the evening, which, of course, he had no intention of doing, and saying "Good-night" good-mannerly enough, he slinked off, and the freshman took his friend up the stairs, which smelled of damp carpets.

The next night Buckley got his gang together. They blew smoke in one another's faces and decided that a little exhibition of oarsmanship in a basin of water with toothpicks would do to warm up with. Then a cross-country jaunt would be appropriate, running, walking, and crawling to the canal. Here, as the freshman was proud of his shape, he would be given an opportunity of displaying it while the moon reflected in the water. And, if he felt cold after that, he could climb a telephone pole for exercise—they didn't want to be inconsiderate of his comfort—and sing "Nearer my home to-day, to-day, than I have been before," at the top of it. Then with a few recitations and solos on the way back he could be put to bed. This would be a good night's work.

It was nearly two o'clock when they carried the ladder into the alley-way. They laid it down in silence.

For several reasons this was to be a right nervy go. A young professor and his young wife had a suite of rooms in the house. But it wasn't that which troubled them. This was. The moon shone full and strong upon the clear, blank wall of the house, and it was in plain view from a certain spot a distance of about two blocks away. Across this spot a certain owl-eyed proctor was pretty sure to pass and repass off and on all night.

That was the reason they were sitting on the ladder waiting for a signal from Colston, who was over by the certain spot watching for the certain proctor.

"Buck, which is the freshman's room?"

"It was the one next to the light and the light was in the room over the side-door."

"Second or third story?"

"Sist! not so loud. Why, let's see, the third."

"Yes," said Haines, "don't you see the window's open up there. None of the family would do that. Town people would never air———"

"Listen!"

A whistle came from the silent distance, the first bar from "Rumski Ho," then a silence, then the same bar repeated. And by this they knew that the proctor had walked into the open space and out of it again, and that if they hurried they could put the ladder against the house, send a man up it and take it away again before the proctor crossed the open space once more.

Buckley started up. The others leaned against the bottom round to steady it. Then he came back for a moment. "Don't take it away until I get all the way in—until I wave my hand. There's plenty of time. Keep cool," he whispered, as he nimbly began his ascent. For his descent he was to rely upon the stairs, the freshman, and his own persuasive powers, for what are freshmen and stairs made for?

Buckley was a right devilish young man, and typically a sophomore. The year before he had climbed the belfry of old North and stolen the bell-clapper and gained class-wide renown. Already this term he had mounted the water-tower and painted the freshman numerals green. The very night before this he had run around the eaves of Reunion, which is no easy trick, with "Bill," the night proctor, behind him, and when he dropped off the bottom round of the fire-escape into the arms of another proctor, he had wriggled out again. Still there are sensations peculiar to scaling a ladder stretching toward the black of an open window, with a moon throwing shadows of yourself and the rounds of the ladder against the dull bricks of an old-fashioned house, while old North strikes two in the distance. Buckley felt them.

The ladder did not quite reach, and he had to stand on the top round and stretch for the sill. Then he pulled himself up, got one foot over, took a longer grip on the inside of the window, dragged the other foot up, as you would climb a high board fence, and was in the room with both feet. He leaned out and waved his hand. The top of the ladder silently swung out from the wall and swooped down in silence. Buckley turned and started across the room.

He could feel the heavier atmosphere of indoors. A small clock was ticking somewhere. He detected a faint scent of mouchoir powder, and was just remarking to himself half consciously that it was just like that pretty-faced freshman, when from somewhere there came a soft voice, saying, "Is that you, dear?"

Then, before all the blood near his backbone had time to freeze into little splinters of ice, he said, "Shsss," and stepped out of the moonlight and into the shadow, which is the best thing to do in case you are ever in a similar situation. Buckley's instinct made him do it.

Across the silence the soft voice floated again and mingled with the moonlight, "Oh, I'm not asleep. But why did you stay so long, Guy, dear?" There was another sound. It was the squeaking of a bed-spring.

Then, as Buckley's knees stiffened tight against each other, he spied coming toward him something white, with two black streaks hanging half way down, which as the thing came into the moonlight, he saw to be long braids of dark hair. Also, the light showed a tall, slender figure clothed in but one garment, which was white, and a face which was young and beautiful. Buckley had never seen a woman dressed that way before, and he closed his eyes.

But he felt it coming nearer and nearer. He stood up perfectly straight and rigid in the darkness as two arms reached up and met about his neck. The arms were soft, and they smelt good.

Buckley did not budge, and the soft voice began, in a sort of whisper, "You have not forgiven me yet?" It began to sob, and he felt the sobbing against his orange and black sweater. "You know I did not mean it. Won't you—forgive her? Won't you forgive—her?" And Buckley fully realized that he was in the thick of some romantically ghastly mistake, and that the only thing he could do to make it worse would be to speak or show his face.

For fully half a minute he stood thus motionless, with his arms at his sides, gathering himself together, and trying to think what to do. And when he had made up his mind what to do he gritted his teeth and put both arms about the Clingy Thing.

And when he had done that the Clingy Thing began to purr in soft, plaintive tones, which undoubtedly were sweet, and would probably have been appreciated by Buckley if he had not been so rattled. "Tell me that you *do* forgive me. Say it with your own lips."

Buckley said nothing with his lips. He was biting them.

"Guy, speak to me!"

Buckley didn't.

"Speak to me, my husband!" A soft, fragrant hand came gently up along his cheek, which tingled, and over his eyes, which quivered, and pushed back the hair from his brow, which was wet. Suddenly she raised her head, gave one look at his face with large, startled eyes, then, with a shuddering gasp, she recoiled.

But Buckley was not letting go. This is what he had been preparing for. Keeping one arm about her waist he threw the other around the neck in such a way that he could draw it tight if necessary, and said in one breath, "For heaven's sake, don't scream—I can explain!"

"Ugh! Oh, let go! Who—let me go or I'll screa-ch-ch-ch."

But Buckley didn't let her do either. He pressed on the windpipe, feeling like three or four kinds of murderers as he did so. Then, as she struggled with feeble, womanly might, Buckley did the fastest thinking he had ever done in all his nineteen years. The door of the room—was it locked? The stairs—where were they? The front door—was the night-latch above the knob? Was it below? Would it stick? All this time she would be screaming, and the house was full of men. He would be caught. He was in for something. But was he hurting her? He began to talk.

"Oh, please, if you scream it'll only make things awfully awkward. I got in here by mistake. I can explain. I'm not going to hurt you. Oh, please, keep quiet."

She tried again to wrench away from his grasp, and Buckley drew her back with ease, feeling half sorry for her poor little strength. "Promise me you'll not cry out and I'll let go."

"Yes, yes, I promise," said the scared voice. "Anything. Only let me go."

Buckley released his grasp. She fled across the room. He thought she was making for the door. He sprang toward it to keep her from running downstairs and arousing the house. But she only snatched up an afghan or something from the sofa, and holding it about her retreated to the dark part of the room.

Buckley couldn't see her now, but he heard her moan, "Oh dear, oh dear!" in a muffled tone, and he felt that she must be cowering in the corner farthest away from him, and it made him have all sorts of contempt for himself. Then he talked again, standing with his back against the door and looking toward the dark. "I don't know who you are," he began in a loud, nervous whisper, "but whoever you are, I wish you wouldn't cry. Please be calm. I want to talk to you."

"I don't want to hear you—I don't want to hear you."

"Not so loud, or we'll be heard."

"Oh, oh, how can you trade upon my necessity? Haven't you a grain of manhood, a spark of kindness in you——"

"Yes, yes, lots," said Buckley. "Listen to me. Please listen. It's all a big mistake. I thought I was coming to my own room——"

"Your own room!"

"I mean my classmate's room—I mean I thought a freshman roomed here. I wouldn't have made the mistake for anything in the world. You aren't half as sorry I got in your room as I am—Oh, yes, you are!—I mean I'm awfully sorry and wish to apologize, and I hope you'll forgive me. I didn't mean anything———"

"Mean anything!"

"Really I didn't. If you'll only let me go down and promise not to wake the house before I get out, why, no one will ever know anything about it, and I'll promise not to do it again. I'm awfully sorry it happened." Buckley started for the door.

"Mrs. Brown—Mr. Brown, help! murder!"

"Oh, for heaven's sake don't!" cried Buckley.

"I will. Just as soon as I get breath and strength enough I mean to wake the house, the neighbors, the whole town if I can."

"No, you won't!" Buckley started across the room.

"Stop!" she cried.

He stopped. The voice was commanding. It seemed already quite strong enough to scream. He said: "You promised not to scream."

"But you forced me to promise."

"Are you going to scream?"

"I am." She was getting her breath.

"Oh, don't; please don't. If I wanted to, I could hurt you. I don't want to hurt you. Ah, have pity on me!"

The bold, bad sophomore was down on his knees, with his hands clasped toward the dark, where the voice came from. He was very sorry for himself.

"You stay right there in the moonlight."

"Right here?"

"Right there. And if you dare to move, I'll scream with all my might."

Buckley first shivered and then froze as stiff as if a hair-trigger rifle were pointing at him. "How long must I stay here?" he asked, without moving his head.

"Until my hus— Until daylight," returned the voice.

"Until daylight!" repeated Buckley. There was something impressive in the deep, rich voice of this tall young woman, and whoever she was, Buckley could tell, from the refined tones, that she was a lady. He could just make out the gleam of her face and of one arm in the dark corner.

Outside, the crickets were scratching in the warm, still night. It was after two o'clock. A moon was shining in his left eye. And he, William Buckley, was kneeling, with his hands stretched imploringly toward a girl whom he had never seen before, in the third story of an old-fashioned Princeton house, which he had entered for the first time by a ladder which, by this time, was resting serenely against a freshly painted house in Mercer Street, whither it had been borne by four classmates, who were now at the corner of Canal and Dickinson Streets, as per agreement, and cursing him for taking such a long time to pull one small freshman out of bed. Meanwhile, the moon was approaching the window-post.

"Please, oh, please, whoever you are," he began, in earnest, pleading tones, "won't you forgive me, and let me go?"

There was no answer.

"I am a gentleman. Indeed I am! I wouldn't harm a girl for the world. Please let me go. I'll be fired—I mean expelled from college for this. I'll be disgraced for life. I'll——"

"Stop!" The voice seemed to be calm now. "While it may be true that you did not break into my room with intent to rob or injure a defenceless woman, yet, by your own confession, you came to torment a weaker person. You wanted to haze one of the freshmen in this house; that was it. And when my husband——"

"Oh, have mercy on me. Won't you have mercy?" Then he began to tell her what a good boy he had always been, and how he had always gone to church, and how fond his mother was of him, and that he was the pride and ambition of the family, and similar rot, showing how completely scared to death he was. "Just think what this means to me," he concluded. "If I'm fired from college, I'll never come back. I'll be disgraced for life. All my prospects will be blighted, my life ruined, and my mother's heart broken."

She gave a little hysterical sob, as if the strain were too great for her. "Yes, for your poor mother's sake; yes, go!" she exclaimed.

"Oh, thank you with all my heart. My mother would, too, if she could know. I don't deserve to be treated so well. I shall always think of you as my merciful benefactress. I can never forgive myself for causing you pain. Oh, thank you."

Buckley, the sophomore, who had strode into that room so manfully, in the full pride of his sophomorish strength and orange and black, grovelled across the room and out of the door, then tip-toed his way down the hall stairs, silently pulled back the latch of the front door, and sneaked off, with his tail between his legs.

The outside air did him good, and by the time he reached his impatient class-mates he had thought up a fairly good lie about the freshman's being ill, quite seriously ill, and about his stopping to look after him a bit, which they admitted was the only thing to do under the circumstances, though it was blamed hard lines, after all the trouble they had taken. "Better luck next time, Buck," they said, and went to bed.

By the ten o'clock mail next morning Buckley received a letter in strange handwriting. It said: "Just as a tall woman looks short in a man's make-up, so does a short man look tall in a woman's make-up, and you should know that blondes are hard to recognize in brunette wigs. I could have done more artistic acting if you had come up earlier, when I had on my full costume. You ought to know that a real girl wouldn't have behaved quite that way. You see you still have a number of things to learn, even though you are a soph. Sort of hard luck, all this, isn't it, old man? Hoping that the rouge will wash off your lips and that you will learn to forgive yourself, I am your merciful benefactress, H. G. Valliant."

This is the freshest thing I ever heard of.

There was a P. S. which said: "Whether or not this thing gets out rests entirely with you and your hazing friends."

Of course it did get out, as all such things do; but Valliant was not bothered again by sophomores, though he ought to have been hazed up and down and inside-out and cross-wise by the whole college.

You can see him if you attend the next production of the Dramatic Association.

HERO WORSHIP

Near Old Chapel he used to linger on the way from recitations, buying things from old black Jimmie and pretending to be amused by his stuttering conversation while he watched the passers-by. And when The One came along for whom he waited, he said to himself, "Oh, he's wearing his brown shooting-coat to-day," and turned and gazed after him until out of sight, wondering what lecture he had at that hour and how he would get along at it. Then passing on slowly across the campus he turned out upon the street.

When he reached his room, Darnell said to another freshman that lived in the house, "I saw Lawrence to-day. He was walking with his arm around Nolan. He passed right by me." And he could also have told just how he nodded to the fellows along the walk and how he swung his legs. Darnell thought that Lawrence's gait was just right. So was his manner of dressing. Somehow Darnell could not make his corduroy coat hang in that way. It lay back all right, but it would not stay snugly up on his shoulders as Lawrence's did.

He used to see him quite often now, for by this time he had learned at what hours Lawrence's lectures came. Which was more than the senior himself knew, for he had always to look at the schedule tacked up on the back of the door over the faculty and absence committee summonses.

Darnell remembered the first time he saw Lawrence. It was on the morning of the first day of the term, while he was sitting in the office of the old Nassau Hotel, quietly waiting for his mother and trying not to appear green and thinking that everyone who came in was a sophomore and wanted him. It was raining, he remembered, and people came scurrying in with their trousers turned up and mackintoshes on. Lawrence came in alone.

He came with his impressive stride and a very long paddock coat and a new kind of shooting-cap which he brought back with him from Piccadilly the first of the month. He frowned and glanced about the room. And when he found the two faces he was looking for and strode across to where a worried-faced gentleman in a silk hat was reading the paper beside a freshman with a grinning face, he said, holding out his hand, "So you have arrived." It was just the patrician tone of voice that Darnell had expected when he saw the face.

When Lawrence stretched out his hand his long coat fell open and disclosed an orange monogram of many closely intertwined letters shining against the black of his undercoat. It was worked upon the breast-pocket, and the freshman wondered what that mysterious insignia might mean.

He watched him as he jerked his head and blew smoke in the damp air. The way he tossed the ashes away was perfect. And when Lawrence suddenly turned and, looking frankly in the freshman's father's eyes, said with a reserved smile, "You need not worry about that, Mr. Jansen," and stretched an arm about the freshman's shoulder, Darnell thought he would rather be that freshman than anyone in the world—except the owner of the arm.

Then he began to speak again, and Darnell found himself leaning forward a little. He remembered thinking, "I don't care if it is impolite to listen."

Lawrence said in a rapid manner, without opening his teeth very wide, "The team? We brought them down from the island last evening. Sea air is a good tonic to begin a season's training with, and they are all in excellent shape. Billy, you must bring your father down to the field to see my big brown babies." Darnell remembered every word, though he did not understand quite what it meant at the time.

Soon after getting settled he took pains to pick up an acquaintance with this freshman. That was the time he first found out that the senior was one of the Lawrences. The freshman said, "Yes, he's a mighty fine fellow. He played on his class eleven in his freshman year." But that was all Jansen said. He did not enthuse as he should have. He had no more than the ordinary fear and reverence of a freshman for a senior. There was a man on the team named Stehman. He was the one this freshman turned and gazed after on the campus.

But now Darnell knew more about him than Jansen did. From the last year's "Bric-a-brac" he had learned the senior's club and what committees he was on, and the book opened up now, of its own accord, to the picture of the Glee Club. He could have told you Lawrence's middle name and his street and number at home, and his campus address as well. Whenever the freshman went to night session of Hall he looked up as he went by to see if the room in West were lighted, and he wondered what he was doing up there behind those curtains. Once, while passing by, some one was calling "Hello-o-o, Harry Lawrence!" and in Lawrence's own voice came a muffled "Hello! Come up." It did not seem quite right for them to be noisy and familiar with Lawrence as with ordinary fellows. He did not understand how Lawrence allowed it.

In Jansen's room it was, and Old North was ringing curfew, when Lawrence shook his hand and said in his peculiar throaty voice, "Glad to know you," or else "Glad to meet you." He never could be certain which it was. It was on a Tuesday evening, and he had made a poor recitation in algebra that day. He noticed that Lawrence was only about an inch taller than himself.

Darnell looked straight back at him and said, "I think I have heard my sister speak of you, Mr. Lawrence. She met you down here at the sophomore reception last June." His voice was perfectly firm and strong, but his mouth persisted in drooping a little at the corners. He could not help that.

Lawrence said, "Yes, I remember very well," which delighted the freshman's sister Louise, when Darnell wrote to her about it, just as much as if it had been true. "Is your sister coming down to any of the dances this year?" added the senior.

"No, I don't believe she is. My aunt brought a whole crowd down that time. Mamma was on the other side, or she would not have allowed it. Louise is not out yet." Then he dropped his big brown eyes and blushed because he felt that he was talking too much and because he had said "mamma" before the senior.

But Lawrence was only looking grave and interested and well-bred, and he replied, "I see. That's too bad. I wish she could come."

"Yes," said Darnell, "I wish she could come," and then, although he did not want to, he arose to go, because he thought that Lawrence wished to talk confidentially with his freshman, Jansen.

Lawrence, who did not care about his going, because he found it as easy to talk to two freshmen as to one, said, "I hope I'm not driving you out, Bonnell. Good-night. If your sister should decide to come down this year, don't forget to let me have a chance at her card before it's filled. Good-night, Bonnell."

"Oh, I won't," said the freshman. "Good-night."

As if he could forget. As if he would be allowed to forget, indeed! She, dear little thing, in her own becoming little way, worshipped him, too. And at Mrs. Somebody's School in Somethingtieth Street, she used to slip an arm about the waist of her latest everlasting friend, and whisper something about it on the way upstairs after prayers.

During her evening's acquaintance with him in June she had told the great, dark, wonderful man that had "a whole tragedy in his face," "a certain indefinable something" in his manner, and many other things, too, no doubt, that she had a brother who was coming to college the next fall, and she asked Lawrence in a very timid, pretty, natural manner if he would please look out for her brother, who would be a freshman and only sixteen years old. And Lawrence, who was watching the way she held her head and approving of it, said, "Of course I will," and forgot about it during the next dance, which was with a Newark girl, who asked him how the Sunday night hot-liquor club was prospering. That was last June.

To be sure Lawrence did not get his name just right, but then many people did not come that near when they first heard it. Besides, what of that? Had he not looked at him and addressed him twice? That was more than most freshmen could say.

But it hurt a little the next day, when Darnell changed his mind about going to the library because he saw that if he kept on up the walk he would meet Lawrence coming toward Dickinson's with three other seniors. For he received only an absent-minded glance without the movement of an eyelash. But you could not expect Lawrence to remember all the people he met. And, perhaps, he was worshipped all the more for it.

On Sunday he used to gaze with his big brown eyes from his seat in the freshman section way over through the juniors and past some of the seniors, back to Lawrence's place. Sometimes a big head of football hair was in the way, so that he could not tell whether he was there. He was absent so frequently. But when they all arose to sing the first hymn, then he could see, and then he would recall what the football column in the paper he had been reading before chapel reported that "President Lawrence" had done or said, and he wondered whether he himself had read it and how it felt to see one's own words in type.

He seldom joined in the singing, Darnell noticed, unless it was "Ein Feste Burg" or "Lead, Kindly Light," and though he could not tell why, Darnell admired him all the more for his not singing every time. At any rate, it was just like him to stand there with his hands in his pockets and his aristocratic head thrown back and look dark and grave and mysterious. He always looked especially so, Darnell thought, in chapel. His mien seemed to be haughty and kingly, not merely dignified and exclusive like that of many upper-classmen. Lawrence when a freshman could never have been hazed or guyed. He could not imagine him stooping to haze anyone either.

Lawrence could do anything. Anyone could see that from his eyes and chin and the straight, firm mouth with the thin lips. Darnell knew very well that Lawrence could stand high in his class if he wanted to. Probably he could play football. He was built well enough. Darnell thought it would not be quite Lawrence's style to play football. He would hate to see him tackled or rolling in the mud. That would never do for him. Lawrence, he thought, would not have played on the team if he were asked. Darnell had been a Princeton man less than a month.

But he had what was far better than playing on the team—the management of it. And he was just right as he was. He was a dignified, weighty senior, respected by all and feared by many, no doubt, and a man, not a boy, who had travelled much and lived much and had had all sorts of experiences in his younger days. He was old now, nearly twenty-two.

But the most wonderful thing about him was his composure and his commanding reserve. He had the look of the gentleman. His manner seemed altogether impervious to excitement. He was master of every situation. To have such a man in their classes must have been rather embarrassing to the professors. Darnell supposed that the other Lawrences were rather afraid of him when he came home.

His perfect command of himself and of everyone and of everything about him was what most impressed the freshman. That was the reason that when his idol fell, it jarred him.

On Thanksgiving evening his head was throbbing and his ears ringing with the echo of horns and cheers, and before his eyes were flashing little kodak recollections of how the line looked when the ball was put in play, and how the crowd waved and yelled when the full-back tried for a goal. But there was a lot of aunts and cousins and things-in-law for dinner, whom he had to kiss and smile at when they said, "How you have grown!" He wanted to get near some class-mate and put his arm about him and talk it all over, like any other healthy young man after the game. And, as early as he decently could, he slipped on his big new coat and stole out by the basement door.

He walked down the avenue to Madison Square, getting jostled and excited once more. Noisy gangs of fours and eights and dozens were marching and dancing along the street. Some wore orange, others blue. Some were students at various colleges, most of them had never seen one.

He went into the Hoffman. Closely packed streams of men were crowding in and out. The air was hot and there was a confused din of many voices. He worked his way to the end of the glaring room, but saw none of his intimates and but few fellows that he had ever seen before. Most of the crowd were of the sort he had seen on the street, young men of the town with college ribbons all over them, and such boisterous noises grated on him, so he started out again. Some hoarse cheering and husky laughter made him turn and look toward the corner where the throng was thickest. Then he hurriedly pushed his way through the crowd to gain a nearer view of what he saw upon the table.

He tried to persuade himself that it was someone else. He did not understand how he could be among people of this sort.

But there was no mistaking that mouth, though he had never seen the hair hanging down that way, nor the eyes as they were now. About the neck was the rim of a hat.

Suddenly two other fellows brushed past Darnell. He looked up and thought he remembered having seen their faces on the campus. They seemed to be excited, and they wedged their way roughly through the crowd to the table. "Leave him alone," one of them was calling out above the din. Brushing aside some slight interference, they picked up the heap from the table, half carried it through the crowd, saying, as they went along, "You're all right, Harry. Brace up, Harry, you're all right," and paying no attention to the crowd, they hurried across the room to the Twenty-fourth Street entrance and disappeared.

For a moment the freshman only stared at a long, tall clock and wondered. Then he suddenly turned and hurried out into the street.

It was no affair of his. The others were there. They were the ones to take care of him. But the electric light had given him one glimpse, and for the moment it was very revolting. He turned and walked slowly home.

He tried to reason himself out of it. It was nothing to feel so queer over. It was not such a terrible thing, after all, especially after having the game turn out as it did. Most every young man was indiscreet at some time or other. Lawrence was a young man like many others, only he happened to have been indiscreet under unfortunate circumstances. That was all. It seemed worse than it really was.

But he did not want Lawrence to be like others. That was just the point. If it had been someone else he would not have cared. But for Harry Lawrence, Lawrence the superb, his Lawrence, there in that glaring place— jeered at and made a fool of—by that mob of muckers. It was all wrong.

"Well," he said to himself, as he went upstairs to his room, "I suppose I'm too much of a kid, and I'll have to get over my kid ways of looking at things. The sooner the better."

But all the same, it hurt, and when he was dropping off to sleep, he was startled into wakefulness again by one of those queer, sudden pangs which make one ask, "What is it I've lost?"

THE RESPONSIBILITY OF LAWRENCE

I

Many fellows seem to think that all an athletic officer has to do is to look important and travel about the United States with his team and make out a bill for expenses.

It's easy enough to carry a japanned tin box, and sell tickets through a hole where the wind blows, as treasurer. As president it is a fine thing to make frequent trips to New York, and attend conclaves that are secret, and make speeches in conventions and read your opinions next morning in the paper in fine long sentences prefixed with "President So-and-so said last night," and to be lunched by famous authorities and interviewed by rapacious reporters who think that because the public supports football they have a right to see all the inside workings of intercollegiate diplomacy. All this is the pretty part of it.

But like all greatness there is a deal of hard hustling and perspiration and discouragement and annoyance underneath. So much so, that one seldom has time to tell himself how fine a thing it is to wear a 'varsity blazer with the orange monogram on the breast-pocket. And this is usually heavy with bills to pay and memoranda of things to see to. Besides, the responsibility is tremendous.

H. Lawrence, Ninety Blank, had blood-shot eyes this morning, and he hurried down the clattering iron stairs of West College tying his neck-tie. As the ugly entry door slammed behind him he did not put his hands in his pockets and begin to whistle, as he used to do in under-classman days, because he was not sauntering over to Reunion to smoke a pipe, or down to Witherspoon to loaf until the next lecture. He glanced at the clock in old North tower and hit up his pace.

He had given orders to the team to be at the station with their grips packed at 9.38, and before that time he had to wire a member of the Graduate Advisory Committee, asking where he could find him that evening, and to an official of the Manhattan Athletic Club that he should not be able to consider his proposition at present, and to the manager of a Southern college football team that he regretted that all Princeton's open dates were now filled, and to the Jersey City Station restaurant to prepare a luncheon of training food for twenty men, and not to roast the beef to death this time. After that he would have to call upon the dean and find out whether the faculty had decided to let Harrison play football or not, and find and be nice to another member of the faculty who was indignant because seventeen grand stand tickets had not been saved for him and his wife's relatives at the last Saturday's game, and then hurry to the station by way of the bank, where he would ask if they had heard anything more about that protested check, while he was making a good one out for himself, and then see to it that all the team and subs were flocked together and pushed into the train and made to stay there until told to get out and play football. Some of which would have been more properly the duties of Sinclair, the treasurer, who was not catching on as rapidly as Lawrence thought he should.

He took long, strong strides and looked straight ahead of him, which was in the direction of an old shop opposite the gate, with a picturesquely warped roof which he did not see.

He did not see the fellows along the walk either, and those he did not cut he nodded to absently without removing his frown. This caused certain passers-by to shake their heads and say, "Harry Lawrence is getting a swelled head since he's become so important," especially those who greatly wanted to be important themselves but weren't, and so had plenty of time to criticise those who were.

But Lawrence, with a half dozen unopened letters in his pocket which he would read on the train going up, did not dream of being criticised. And if he had he would not have felt very badly about it. He did not have time.

Nor would he have had time to stop and thank his good friends Nolan and Linton, who, when Lawrence had rushed by with one of those "How-do's" which make one think that one's name has been forgotten, had looked worried and then said, "Harry'll kill himself before the end of the season," while Lawrence tore open a telegram with which the boy met him in front of College Offices and hurried on. He had no time for breakfast, because the man had forgotten to wake him, and the night before he had been handling the files of applications for the Thanksgiving game seats with Sinclair and dictating to a stenographer until 2 A.M.

Every evening from eight until midnight there was a reception in his room, with Sinclair to help receive. It began when they came in from the club after dinner, with a workman or two from the town waiting in the entry, who touched their hats and said, "Please, sir, Mr. McMaster says this bill is correct." Then would come members of the team who wanted the management to remove conditions for them, and coachers who wanted to talk serious business and had but a short time to spare, and some of the fellows who wanted to smoke and chat and seemed hurt when told to get out; and in addition, the hordes of applicants for seats, who kept running in and out, incessantly buzzing in the management's ears like flies, and just as pestiferously merciless, from eight until twelve, when the door was locked.

These represented all phases of college life, from the professor who "never incurred any difficulty in getting all the seats he wanted in previous years" to the young freshman whose mother knew the management's mother, and thought he might be especially considered for that reason, and including class-mates who made it a personal matter of friendship, and thought they ought to be considered ahead of mere strangers for that reason. Also emissaries from a certain woman's college, who must have tickets before they are put on sale, because the poor, timid girls could not stand in line with all those men, and cousins of members of the team, and many others, all of whom furnished an excellent reason for being entitled to just a little more consideration than anyone else. None of which counted them anything in Lawrence's reign.

But this was not what made Lawrence scowl and look fierce as he hurried by a little, wistful-eyed freshman, whom he did not see, and who had been hoping all the way from the First Church gate to the dean's that maybe this time the senior would recognize him. Lawrence was used to all this, and he liked it. He liked having a lot of things to attend to in a short time, to see many people and give orders and talk fast and feel his brain warm with quick thinking. He enjoyed responsibility, and he thought it was thrilling to get in a situation and then take a long breath, so to speak, and command it. Nor was he too old to fully appreciate his privilege of being on intimate terms with ancient heroes of the football field, and he was glad to be thrown with so many other prominent alumni. And he took great satisfaction in watching the long-headed Advisory men begin to acknowledge by their attitude that although an undergraduate he had reliable executive ability and somewhat of independent resource besides. One of them clapped him on the back one day and said, "Good! That's the proposition we'll make 'em," and added, "You are your father's own son, Lawrence."

Except that he would have liked to have a little time to loaf and enjoy life, he was quite well pleased with being president of the P. U. F. B. A., and did not care a rap whether the college considered him arrogant or not. He was attending to his own business and had the satisfaction of knowing that he was doing it rather well, with the attendant satisfaction of having had the honorable position given him by the vote of the college body without his or his friends' boot-licking one of them for it. And that is one of the most satisfactory feelings in the world.

The thing that troubled him was a letter in his pocket. That was the reason that when the ninth old grad. approached him on the field and said, "Say,

Lawrence, just between us now, what do you think of the chances with Yale?" he replied, curtly, "How do I know?" and hurried on up the side lines. This was decidedly fresh, and he jumped on himself afterward because he did not believe in letting private affairs interfere with business. Usually he could stand a dozen old graduates.

The letter had come the day before. It was from his father and enclosed Lawrence's November allowance. He never received but one letter a month from the governor, and it nearly always contained two statements: "Enclosed please find ..." and "Your mother and all are well," both of which make very agreeable reading.

This time the letter was not dictated, but written in the Colonel's own small, straight hand, and there was an extra paragraph. It ran thus: "Had I known what this official position of yours involved, the amount of time, the number and variety of interruptions, and the vulgar prominence that your name and movements occupy in the press, I should never have given my consent, which, as you may remember, I did reluctantly, to your acceptance of it. In my opinion what you are learning at college could better be acquired at home: a little of business down-town with me, your *other accomplishments* up-town in the clubs and other places with your friends." This was not the sort of letter to do any good.

"'Your other accomplishments'—now what the devil does he mean by that, I wonder?" thought Lawrence. And then he folded the letter and tossed it into a pigeon-hole marked "Unanswered," and turned his attention upon a large blue-print marked "Stand B" and tried to assure himself that the reason his mind kept jumping back to pigeon-hole "Unanswered" was because he was sorry at being too busy to study, and disliked having such a low stand in class. But it wasn't his class standing that kept him awake until old North struck five.

After this when in New York he did not go up-town to dine with the family as often as formerly. When he did his father merely said, "Judge Hitchcock told me he saw you on Broadway last Wednesday," and similar remarks in a casual tone.

"Yes, sir," Harry would reply, with his attention on the crest on his plate.

Then each would wonder what the other meant, until Helen would interrupt with, "By the way, I saw by the *Tribune* this morning that 'President Lawrence of Princeton' says that Yale will beat Harvard at Springfield. So it's all right then, Winston." He was her husband, Yale '86, and Helen was a good sister, who had a large intuition and knew things.

On Thanksgiving Day the College of New Jersey went up to New York feeling quite certain of winning the game. The alumni said we would win.

The heelers doubled their bets. The coachers were sure we'd win. Most of the authorities conceded the victory to Princeton. The team were confident of winning. Yale won.

During the dinner after the game, Lawrence was dignified and silent. People thought he was rattled, if anyone thought about anything else than the one big, sad fact. He presided gracefully though. He was very good to look at. The dinner, which is usually very long, was wound up early, few being unwilling, and Lawrence helped put one of the blubbering backs to bed who had taken too much for a training stomach and head. Then he went downstairs, saying, "Now, then, my responsibility is over with. I am going to have a good time."

II

He had done it hard because he did everything hard. It had lasted several days and ended in a hospital in West Philadelphia, where he had three stitches put in his forehead. Now he was back in his old room in West College, with a pipe in his mouth, drumming on the arms of his chair and staring straight at his feet, which were upon the roller-top desk. Dark rings were under his eyes and he told himself that he had had a good time.

He was thinking that it was quite a storybook coincidence that they should have come together, those two letters. They were so different and yet so much the complement of each other.

The first was from his father. He had torn it open with his pen, as he would any other letter, and though he saw that it was several pages in length and knew intuitively that it would not be like any other letter he had ever read, he had deliberately rolled up the envelope to get a light for his pipe from the fire, and he had stretched out in the chair again as he was before, with his legs sprawled out in front and elbows resting on the arms, holding the letter before his face.

Then he had commenced to smoke very hard, and presently stopped rocking back and forth as he read the words written in that clear, even hand, without a flourish or a superfluous mark, words that had caused him to gnaw the mouth-piece of his pipe as they burned their way into him. And all the while he pictured to himself a tall figure in a smoking-jacket trimmed with white braid sitting up straight and rigid at his desk in the corner of the cosey inner room of the office in William Street, and recalled how once, when an absconding clerk had left a temporary cloud on the name of the firm, the old, steely eyes had flashed under the lowering brows as the old gentleman had taken his seat at the breakfast-table, where he ate nothing.

The letter sounded very like the governor. There was no mistaking its meaning. It was a succinct and comprehensive report of dissatisfaction at the younger Lawrence's methods, with a list of debts of filial affection and memoranda of overdraws on parental patience covering the last three years, and accompanied by a brief prospectus for the unpromising future. It was the sort of a letter he would have fancied a stately old gentleman like his father that was proud of his name writing to a son like himself that had disgraced it.

Only it would have been just as well, Lawrence thought, to have omitted that part of the letter. He was quite willing to admit most of the hard things his father said of him because they were facts, but this about dishonorable cowardice and the family name was going a little too far, and he told himself that he did not quite see how he could stand that from anyone. And he sat up straight and pressed hard on the arms of his chair and looked very like the indignant old Colonel who had written the words.

It was uncalled for, it was unjust, it was ridiculous. If his father would stop to think of things as they really were in this world, thought Lawrence, Ninety Blank, these little shortcomings of his would not appear a bit worse than those of some of the very same young men in town whose industry and clean business ability the Colonel so much admired, and whom he spoke of as the hope or flower or something of Manhattan's commercial supremacy or something.

It was merely that he happened to be indiscreet the last time he was having a good time. He had made a little too much noise, and the echo had reached a number of people in town. That was all. It was hard luck, but it did not amount to enough to become dramatic over. Merely because his great-grandfather did something and his grandfather was something was no reason, as far as he could see, why the Lawrences should have unique moral standards. The governor was certainly getting old.

Then he had carefully arranged the leaves of the letter in order, mechanically folded and put them in a pigeon-hole of the desk, and opened and spread out the other letter before him. But he did so unconsciously, for he was staring straight out ahead of him into the face of the future, which had expressionless features. His father had concluded with "Signify to me at once your intention of a complete change in your career, or, notwithstanding your nearness to graduation, I shall take you out of college and put you at work in Van Brunt's." That is not the way a boy likes to be written to.

"Oh, no, I don't think I'd do all that if I were you." He could not abide his father's tone when he spoke of *taking* him out of college or *putting* him at work, or doing anything with him. He was still young enough not to fancy being considered young.

And then the actuality of the situation occurred to him, and he was reminded that although twenty-one he had not a cent of his own, and that there was no place in the world to go to or a thing that he could do to make money enough to even pay his debts.

"Picture of a young man taken out of college because he is bad." He smiled broadly at himself in the glass over the mantelpiece. But it wasn't very funny.

And it was at this point that he dropped his eyes to read his father's words once more, and was startled for an instant to see a strange handwriting, and then remembered the other letter. He was again startled by the first words that met his glance. "Haven't you had enough of college?" At the top of the paper was the name of a La Salle Street, Chicago, firm. It was not so very queer after all. It was only that it was so startlingly apropos. He read the letter in eager gulps. Then he read it again.

It was from his friend Clark, who had been so kind to him when he was out there. And now he was still more kind. It was singular that the offer should come just now, on that very day, at that very hour. He would wire back his acceptance that afternoon. "Now, of course, it is too bad to make you stop in the middle of your last year," the letter ran, "but we can't hold it open after the first of January. I know what a big concession you consider it for a New Yorker to come to Chicago, but you know better than to be prejudiced. You know the crowd you'll blow with and the clubs you'll be in, and as the situation is something extraordinary to be offered to so young a man, I hope you'll wire me your acceptance at once. The mature judgment you showed in conducting...." These words came to his heated brain like a cool lake-breeze. This was what he wanted more than anything else in the world just now, to get away from his present surroundings, and to start anew, where he would be his own master, making his own money and disposing of it as it suited him, and responsible to no one for the use he made of it or his time. He wanted to be free.

The bell in Old North broke in on him. He looked at the clock on the mantelpiece, and was surprised to see that it was only four, and that it must have been but a half hour since he received those two letters. Then he remembered that he had a lecture at that hour. It made him smile to think of it.

But, it occurred to him, it would be a right good idea to go—he would be going to few enough more—anything to get out of the close atmosphere of the room and interrupt the current of his thought. For his thoughts were chasing each other about in a circle, and they would not stop, although he pressed his forehead with both hands, as he used to do during the football season. Lately his brain had taken to behaving in a very queer manner, and a fellow he knew at the College of Physicians and Surgeons had told him that if he did not stop worrying about things he would have neurasthenia or something as ugly sounding as that.

As he opened the entry door and stepped out into the open air of the campus, the old bell began throbbing, clear and strong, in his ears. It somehow recalled freshman year and how he used to run to reach his seat before it stopped ringing.

He was in the crowded quadrangle now, with fellows all about him with books or note-books under their arms, whistling and singing and hallooing and scraping their feet along the walks just as they had always done. Over in front of Reunion was the usual crowd kicking football and squabbling over their points. The side over by College Offices was shouting exultingly "Nine to seven!" and a fellow on the side near by was announcing with equal conviction, as he turned the ball over in his hands to punt, "Eight to seven." Lawrence found himself saying "Eight to seven," and mechanically watched the ball as it sailed through the air and lodged up in one of the second-story balconies, and stopped to listen to them set up the cry, just as he knew they were going to, "Thank you, up there, please, thank you-u-u!"

It struck him as queer that all this was going on just as it always had, without a single variation to show that this day was different from other days. It seemed odd to think that he was not to be a part of this any more. It somehow seemed more odd than sad. He told himself that it would be a great relief to fly far away from it all.

Down the walk came a group of his own class-mates, carelessly slouching along from lecture, laughing and joking, with their arms on one another's shoulders. It was Linton and Nolan and Stehman and others. "Hello, there, Harry!" they said and passed on down the walk. Lawrence turned and watched them. He had replied to their salute in his usual manner. It had seemed natural and his voice was in perfect imitation of heartiness, and yet he could not help thinking how little difference it would make to him if they all fell down dead. The sight of them bothered, Nolan's bow legs annoyed him. He hoped he would never see Nolan again. And this was Billy Nolan!

The bell was echoing and re-echoing in his ears, and each stroke fairly made him jump. The sight of so many people and the knowledge that there were others behind him were beginning to give him a feeling of distress. He felt that he could not stand having so many people press close to him. It was somehow rattling him. Everything he saw hurt, and he only wanted to get far away from it all. For he told himself that he hated the campus and its life, and everything that had to do with it. The very expression of the buildings was offensive to him. He wanted to upset the wheelbarrow and its sticky contents when old black Jimmie touched his hat to him, and he felt like kicking two innocent seminoles that hurried past with quick, conscientious steps that made their coat-tails flap behind. All of this was nervous nonsense, and he knew it.

He left the crowded walk and walked over toward the cannon and leaned against a nearby elm-tree. Then he fixed his gaze steadily upon the top of the old cannon and tried to think of nothing else. He had learned to take himself in hand this way during his overworked football season. "It isn't so bad as all this," he said aloud to himself. "You are still rocky and your blamed nerves are getting in their work again. That's all it is. Now, then, hold on. You aren't a hysterical little school-girl, you know."

In a moment he started on toward Dickinson Hall again. "We are going to a lecture now," he explained to himself in a whisper, "and we're going to hear lots of interesting things. We can talk over all those other matters later on. There's plenty of time, plenty of time."

He took a long, full breath, as though to hold on tight, and threw up his head and looked squarely into a pair of brown eyes that were gazing intently at him. It was That Freshman.

He had often wondered why he was constantly running across this same little freshman with the sensitive mouth and the large, thoughtful eyes. He did not know his name, but he enjoyed observing from the patronizing height of a senior an air of delicate refinement in the features and movements of the boy. Sometimes when in a good humor he nodded to him. But just now the peculiar wistful gaze breaking in on him in his tossed-up state of mind seemed eerie. For an instant he had a feeling of guilty fright, as if caught doing something. And then, because angry with himself for being startled by a freshman, he blurted out, in a husky voice, "Oh, what do you want?"

The under-classman blushed and stepped back. He said something incoherent ending with "Why—er—nothing— I beg pardon." He attempted a smile, failed, colored more than ever, dropped his eyes in embarrassment, and with a sort of shiver turned on his heel.

The senior, with his own harsh voice still echoing in his ear, stood there with his hands in his pockets watching the younger boy shrinking before him. Then something inside of him was touched. He felt how brutally rude he had been, and he wanted to make amends for it. He felt more than that. He wanted to be kind to this boy with the refined face; he wanted to be tender toward him, to protect him, or something queer and wild like that. Though he did not acknowledge it to himself tears were ready to come to his dark, blood-shot eyes with the dark rings under them, and he had an impulse to throw his arm about the freshman's shoulder and say: "You dear little fellow!" Neurasthenia could account for some of this.

As it was he turned and followed the freshman from the side of the new bulletin-elm, where this took place, to the corner of the Old North. Here, hardly realizing what he was doing, he touched his shoulder and said, in a gruff voice, though he did not mean it to be, "Don't you want to take a walk?"

But even if he had stopped to think about its being an odd thing to do, it would have made no difference. He was hardly in a mood for considering conventionalities.

After awhile he found himself walking with the freshman way out toward the Prep. school. To the left was the old view of rolling fields and the gentle hill. Underfoot were the uneven stones of the old walk with water-puddles in the hollowed-out places. And there beside him walked the freshman, talking in a natural tone about a fine tennis-player that he thought was coming to college next year. It was all quite as if it were an ordinary occurrence.

Lawrence could remember the freshman's look of surprise as they started across the campus, and he recollected murmuring some apology for his rudeness by saying that he thought it was someone else at first. Then he must have started the conversation by asking the freshman what recitation he had just had. But after that it was all a blank until now. He was under the impression that he had been nodding to people, but he could not remember who they were or anything about them except a big-visored, faded crimson cap that someone had on. Probably he had been carrying on the conversation automatically with the freshman, but it must have been all right, for the boy did not look as though anything strange had happened. But a very great deal had.

Perhaps it was a sort of hypnotism, though very likely it could be explained as nothing of the kind, but at any rate from the moment his thoughts had been stopped with a jerk at meeting the freshman they had taken a different turn. With the boy at his side and his gentle voice in his ears Lawrence had begun thinking about another red-cheeked boy he had known once; and it seemed much more than four years ago. He felt again the very expression of those old bright days at school when he took prizes and played on the eleven. He remembered the old field and how the afternoon sun used to reflect from one of the windows near by. There came back to him the very odor of the polished desk in the school-room where he scratched H. L. L., and all the little details of those dear old days of happy monotony and innocent amusements. He felt again the old excitement of an approaching vacation. He remembered how he used to check off the days on the calendar over the mantelpiece, and he remembered the first trip he took home alone and the blue serge suit he wore, of which he was so proud, and how he wondered who would meet him at the station, and best of all, how he used to jump out of the carriage and run up the steps of home and meet the one that came out into the hall to meet him. Joyously and innocently he used to look up into the soft gray eyes that seemed to say, "I am proud of my boy." But that was a peculiar thing to think of just now. A passage in his father's letter occurred to him. "Of course I did not, nor shall I advise your mother of all this"—he had had to turn the page, he remembered, to find the rest of it—"it would break her heart." "Of course," he said to himself, hurriedly, "it wouldn't do at all." Then he thought he did not care to dwell upon old times any more. It was at this point that he awoke, so to speak, and found himself walking with this freshman whose name he did not know.

But instead of everything springing back to actuality immediately as one would suppose, it took some time to hammer things into seeming as they really were in their proper proportions. It was like trying to act sober. He began by paying conscious attention to what his young friend was saying.

After all he was only a freshman. He talked like any other fellow except that his voice was more gentle, and he had a deferential manner when addressing him. Though rather young to be in college and of unusual appearance, there was not enough about him to affect a fellow in such a queer sentimental way.

And yet he did. To Lawrence he seemed different from everyone else in the world. He had never experienced this peculiar melting feeling toward anyone before. What was more, he liked it, and he had no thought of laughing himself out of it. He had an undefined idea that it was doing him good. He felt like clinging close to this companion who was younger and seemed so many times better and purer than himself.

Then suddenly the senior was struck by something he had not remarked before. He waited a moment to make sure. Then it came again. There was no mistaking it this time. The refined voice was dragging in profanity at absurdly frequent intervals, with every other sentence almost. He had very likely been doing so all along. And the odd part of this was that every word of it was making Lawrence wince and shiver like seeing a respectable woman drunk. It was none of his business. It was all nonsense. The expletives were not very bad ones anyway. But he did not care to stand any more of this; and as abruptly as he had proposed the walk he said: "Oh, excuse me, I have an engagement," and turned rapidly toward the campus. Perhaps neurasthenia had a hand in this also.

He did not stop to see how the freshman took it. He did not want to think of him now. He fairly ran up Nassau Street with a feeling as though someone was after him. He rushed past the fellows along the walk and nearly bumped into the three old professors starting off with the Irish setter for their sedate evening stroll. He was trembling when he reached his room, and he slammed the door and threw himself down on the rug before the fire.

He knew something was coming. He knew what it was, too, but he was going to fight it off as long as he could. He drew the end of the fur skin up over his head and pressed hard with both hands, as though that would keep him from thinking of what he did not want to think. Then he rubbed the back of his hand across his wet brow and tried to sneer the thing away as he had always been able to do at other times. But this was not at all like any of the other times, and it would not work. Besides his nerves were in no shape for a fight of this sort, and he soon gave up. He let his head fall back against the rug and he lay there flat on the floor while the aching thoughts came soaking over him. All this had been accumulating for many days. The freshman had set it off.

And it was not as if he had only a little to feel sorry over. He could not even say, "I'm no worse than most fellows," for he had gone quite far indeed, much farther than anyone in the world, except two or three, had any idea of, and he had things to remember that very few older sinners than he would often care to think about. It seemed so certain to him now, as he lay there breathing hard and staring at the fire as though expecting it to jump out at him, that these remembrances were never going to let up on him for a single moment; as long as he lived, no matter how he might live in the future, these unforgetable things were, from this time on, to rise up and spoil every bit of sweetness in life for him.

But that was not what hurt the most. It was just and reasonable that all that should be as it was. It was the thought of his people at home that was making him squirm and roll over toward the desk and then back again toward the fire. What had they done to deserve this? He could not understand. Aside from all consideration of right and wrong, or wisdom and folly, he was astounded at the thought of how a fellow could be so dead, dead unkind. It would not seem possible at first. He kept asking himself, "Is this really true? Is it really true?"

For an hour he lay there on the floor, with his remorse and his sick nerves, telling himself the kind of a fellow he was, while the rest of the college went to dinner.

After this came the reaction, the natural instincts of love and yearning for the home that he had left. He told himself how that vacations would come, and little Dick, the prep., would come, and Helen and all would come out there to the old place on Long Island—all but one. His place at the table would be vacant. No, there would be no place for him. They would avoid mentioning his name. They would change the subject when visitors referred to him. After awhile visitors would learn not to refer to him. He would be known as "the one that went to the devil."

All his self-reliance had been squeezed out of him. He did not care to be independent now. He did not want to be free. He wanted—oh, how he wanted!—a place to go to and people to care about him, like everyone else. He shrank from the thought of standing alone. He did not feel equal to it. He felt himself to be nothing but a boy, after all, a bad, foolish, wilful, sick boy, and he wanted to run home and, just for once, let his throbbing head fall into his mother's lap and have her hands smooth the ache out of it. But of course he could do nothing of the sort.

The more he thought of it the more impossible it appeared. Why, for four years—he half arose from the rug and his face became hot at the thought of it—for four years he had been doing things that she would not believe him capable of; not if he told her himself. No, he was not going to sneak into the home-fold like a cowardly prodigal, bleating, "I have been a bad little boy, papa. Take me back, and I'll promise not to be bad any more." He was not that kind. He deserved his husks, and he meant to chew them, even though they stuck in his throat. To keep away, he showed himself, was one means left him to regain a little of the self-respect that he had lost.

Then he arose with something of his former indifference and laughed at himself a little. "You've felt sorry for yourself long enough," he said aloud; "what you've got to do now is to make the best of it." He started toward the desk to take the first steps toward making the best of it. He stopped in the middle of the room and looked about at the pictures and the pipes and the books. "I'm done with college," he said, briskly. "Now I feel better."

He lighted a pipe to show himself how much better he felt, and began to word a telegram to Clark. That would finish a good day's work, he thought. A very long day it seemed, too. Some things were hazy and dream-like. That walk with the freshman— But he did not want to think about that, and he wrote down "W. G. Clark, care West, Houston & Co."

Yet, though he tried not to listen, there began coming up to him the tones of the gentle voice dragging in profanity with such pathetic pains. "But I don't want to think about that!" Lawrence exclaimed. But all the while he wrote the message he heard the timid voice with the incongruous words.

"I wish you wouldn't do that," he said aloud. "It bothers me. Why do you want to do that?" He dipped his pen in the ink and held it there. Why did he? Then it came over him with a blush of shame that it was doubtless to find favor in his sight. Most people would have guessed it before.

And then something flashed through his mind, something that he had heard early in the term. A freshman named Jansen, whom he had looked out for when he first arrived, had told him of a freshman that was always talking and asking questions about him. Lawrence had entirely forgotten this, and the recollection of it made him start up from his seat. This accounted for the freshman's haunting him on the campus, gazing at him, imitating his style of dress even.

It was quite ridiculous. He tried to sneer it out of his mind. But he could not. He was finding that there were some things that could not be sneered away. But that was not all.

A big question met him like a huge, choking wave—"What will this boy's future be?" And Lawrence pleaded, "Oh, let me alone! Never mind all that."

The wave drew back and another came drenching over him—"Will he do as you have done?"

"Don't, please don't!" cried Lawrence. There came up before him in his sick mind lurid, revolting scenes, and in them a fair-faced boy with a sensitive mouth learning to like it all. Then came a third wave—"Who will be responsible? What are you going to do about it?" This was a little too much for Lawrence. He felt powerless to think it out just now. He would need time for this. Unconsciously he stepped back to the rug. He lay there, very quiet, almost motionless, until far into the night.

Then he arose, a very different boy from Lawrence the President, greatly feared of under-classmen, and felt his way through the dark to the bedroom. Here he locked the door and prayed to God, as he had been brought up to do.

The next morning one of the clerks, harrying by the ticker where Colonel Lawrence seemed to be bending over the tape, suddenly exclaimed, "Why, what is it, sir? Nothing serious, I hope?"

Old Colonel Lawrence, drawing himself up and gazing straight ahead of him as he crumpled a telegram in his hand, made answer, "No. My son is coming home to spend Sunday with me. That is all."

The clerk did not know that they were tears of joy.

FIXING THAT FRESHMAN

I

Lawrence, Ninety Blank, wearily knocked four under-classmen off the walk on the way from the railway station to West College. Then, feeling better, he dragged himself up the entry stairs, threw his suit-case at the bedroom portière with a sigh of relief and himself on the divan with a sense of having done his duty.

The Glee, Banjo, and Mandolin Clubs had just returned from their Christmas holiday tour through the South. The trip had been a success both in the money and the fine impression the clubs had made, which latter would advertise the college. And that is the object of this enterprise and is too valuable for the trustees to abolish.

They had travelled in a special train of private cars lent by the parents of some of the members. They had had a very good time, because a Glee club trip is always bound to have that, and because Southern people know how to help young men in this respect about as well as any people in the world. Lawrence was glad it was over.

He had not intended to go on the trip this year. He had been on the club since he was a freshman. He knew all there was to know about it, and there could be little novelty in this sort of thing for him. But that was not the reason.

Of course it was not. Harry Lawrence enjoyed travelling about the country with a rollicking lot of congenial fellows, and being made much of by old grads., and admired before the glare of foot-lights by millions of attractive girls, and dancing with them afterwards until three o'clock in the morning, like any other normal, healthy young man. It was not because he was *blasé*. He wasn't that sort of fool.

In the first place Lawrence had suddenly gone home, early in December, with something pronounced by a little, short doctor with mild blue eyes which saw everything to be a form of neurasthenia. This was brought on by overwork and worry and other causes. He had held a position of considerable responsibility during the football season. He had worried over it a good deal.

Although, when he reached home, he braced up with astonishing rapidity, he conceived a notion that instead of flying over the United States at the rate of ever so many miles an hour, he would like very well to sit still and yawn by the fireplace at home with slippers on.

His mother opened up the old place on Long Island for a part of every winter, and he thought he could put in a very comfortable old-fashioned vacation out there with her. He had an idea that it would do him good to take some long tramps over the meadows with a gun and a dog, and to spend whole afternoons on a horse with pure country air whistling in his ears. Perhaps, if he felt right cocky, he might borrow some pinks of his brother-in-law and ride to the hounds with his Ass-cousins on New Year's Day. And the evenings would pass pleasantly enough in fighting with Helen, his married sister, across the table, and in guying his kid brother Dick, the prep.; and then he meant to have many long after-dinner smoke-talks with his father, with whom he had recently become acquainted. It was on this last account, as much as any, that he wanted to stay at home.

But one of the second basses had the grip and another a dead grandmother, and that side of the stage was weak anyway. So Doc. Devereaux, the leader of the club, followed his two letters and three telegrams out to Compton on the Sound, and grabbed Lawrence by the coat-collar. He had brought with him a reprieve from the little blue-eyed doctor, stating that Lawrence could go if he would promise to keep on with the hot and cold baths, and to eat tremendously. Devereaux begged and pleaded, and put it on grounds of personal friendship. When he shed tears, almost, and said, "For the honor of old Nassau won't you, Harry?" Lawrence looked bored and said he would think about it. But only upon condition that Doc would stay for dinner and spend the night at Compton, which he did.

When Colonel Lawrence came out from town and had comfortably finished his dinner, and in his stately fashion had taken out a long black cigar, Harry, who had been waiting, said, "Now then, father," and told him why Devereaux was there, and asked him what to do about it.

Lawrence, Fifty Blank, knocked the ashes off, looked at Lawrence, Ninety Blank, and took three puffs of smoke. "Well, Harry," he said, "if the college needs you, there is but one way of looking at it." Lawrence, the younger, said "Yes, sir," and packed his suit-case.

Having decided to do his duty, he made up his mind that while he was about it he would enter into the spirit of the thing and have a good time. Of course this was not as satisfactory to himself as wearing a long face and telling himself what a martyr he was, but it was pleasanter for his friends.

These trips are not only good fun, they are part of one's education. They are very broadening. Lawrence wanted to be broad-minded. The only times he had travelled in his own country were with the Glee Club, and he thought every young man ought to know something of his fatherland.

He held that most New Yorkers were narrow-minded in this respect, and he did not intend to be. New York ways of doing things were good enough for him, because they were the best, but he wanted to see how other Americans looked at things; and this showed a generous spirit.

On a previous trip he had visited a portion of the Western section of his country, and had brought back several new ideas. For instance, he was pleasantly surprised to meet girls with the same innate ideas that he had supposed were the exclusive possession of his friends at home. That was broadening. Also he had it impressed upon him that young women living in little towns he had never heard of before had characteristics, not necessarily innate, which were calculated to make very young men realize that even members of college dance committees have a thing or two to learn. Which was still more broadening.

And now he was in Virginia, surrounded by much dazzling full-pulsed Southern loveliness. He was meeting people that had been brought up to consider themselves the aristocracy of the American side of the world, and they had been cherishing this idea for generations before New York was more than a trading-post of miserly, Indian-cheating Dutchmen. They had never heard of the Lawrences of New York and were rather sorry for anyone that had to live there. And this was broadening. This was not to be about the Glee Club trip, nor about what Lawrence would have done if he had not gone, but what happened afterward, and if you read this story you may skip to here: Lawrence lay on the divan.

He put his hands back of his head and tried to tell himself how sick he was of teas and club receptions and convivial old grads. and applause and dances and chicken-salad and girls. Cinders were in his hair. What he wanted most in all the world was, first, someone to carry him to a Turkish bath, second, someone to dress him in his campus clothes, and third, Billy Nolan to put an arm around and call names.

But this reactional feeling he knew was inevitable, and he took it, as he did his sensation of dirtiness and indigestion, as part of the game. There was something else to make him fidget and frown on the divan.

Lawrence had come back to the slushy old sunshiny campus a very different fellow from the one that used to climb the stone steps from the station, but he had had a month in which to become accustomed to it. Besides, that was nothing to be sour about. He was very well pleased with being a different sort of a fellow, and had made up his mind to remain so. In fact, all during the trip he had been thinking that he could put in a peaceful, comfortable time now for the rest of his life, if it were not for one thing.

And as he started across the campus with a roll of corduroys under his arm, and the intention of taking a bath at the club, the very first thing he saw was that One Thing.

There was a "Hunt's Discourse" under his arm, and he was running to reach his seat before the bell stopped ringing, like any other freshman. But he was different from every other freshman in the world, to Lawrence.

This boy, like some of every freshman class that ever cheered itself hoarse, was beginning to do things his father had not sent him to college for. And the senior had an idea that his own example was what had started the boy; and this, when you stop to think of it, was extremely conceited in him. He thought he could make the freshman stop, and this, when you stop to think of it, was a hasty conclusion.

He thought about it during the time occupied in splashing and spluttering at the club, and most of the time that he was shivering and whistling and putting on his ugliest sweater and oldest corduroys and most disreputable slouch hat, and his brown shooting-coat with quail blood on it. He even thought of it several times while his hands were deep down in his pockets and his shoulders were slouched forward and a pipe was in his mouth and an arm was around Jim Linton and they were floating about the campus calling hello to everybody that was back.

The first thing undertaken by Lawrence, the entirely different, was the purchasing of some fine large text-books. For his foremost duty was of course toward himself.

He had never bought any books since freshman year, but he knew where they were to be found, and a poler named Stacy gave him a list of the ones he required.

They were all nice new copies, with the book-store smell about them. He did not like second-handed ones, and then, too, he was going to pole very hard and he might wear them out. Besides, his book bill had never been large—except in his letters—and he thought he could afford the extravagance in his senior year.

He took great pleasure in writing his full name on the fly-leaf with a blotty pen, Henry Laurence Lawrence, Jr., in a flourishless hand like his father's. They made quite an imposing pile on the table, and he felt proud of it. He showed them to the fellows that dropped in that evening to say, "Glad to see you back," and ask him what he thought of Southern girls. This took until 2 A.M. So he could not attend to that other matter until the next day.

He set the alarm-clock before going to bed and said, "Now, then, to-morrow I fix my freshman."

He jumped out with only six hours' sleep, though he had just finished a long journey and his nerves required more rest, all to make chapel and see his freshman. He saw him.

Although he said only, "How do you do?" in a serious tone, he knew that he was doing his duty, and felt so pleased with himself that he went to town that afternoon and took a Turkish bath at his place in Twenty-eighth Street—this was the only way to get the cinders out—and stole some clean linen from his brother-in-law's top bureau drawer, and dined with the family at home. Then, because he had not been with them during Christmas, and because he was to be a poler for the rest of his college course and would have few such chances, he stayed over Sunday and was given a pensum for too many unexcused absences when he came back.

On Monday, however, he saw his freshman again. It was on Nassau Street. This time Lawrence said, "Hello there!" He saw him once more on Tuesday, coming out of Whig Hall, and said, "How are you, Darnell?" and smiled a little. He saluted the freshman in various ways every day but one for a week.

This delighted the freshman very much, but somehow had no effect upon his morals. Lawrence felt like a man wasting breath, and he did not believe in wasting breath on under-classmen. This young Darnell was decidedly unappreciative. Besides it was unwarrantably fresh in him to give all this trouble to a senior, and Lawrence made up his mind to some day tell him so.

If it had been a good hard jumping-on that were needed, Lawrence thought he could have managed, but this thing required tact and delicacy, which he hadn't. Some fellows, like Jim Linton, would not have minded a queer, unconventional situation of this sort. Lawrence was not that kind. He knew as little about telling a fellow that he was on the verge of making a fool of himself as he did about informing people that they had souls, or that they should study hard. It made him blush to think of it.

Besides, what force would this sort of thing have coming from Lawrence, Ninety Blank? That was the disadvantage of having a reputation like his. Nor could he very well halt the freshman on the campus and say, "See here. Stop this. I am a good boy now. You also must be a good boy." Ugh!

The mid-year examinations would be on in a week or two, or three, and for the present he was simply obliged to leave off reforming the freshman—especially as he had decided that it would look nice this time for his report to go home without any conditions on it. It was his duty to pole.

Study, after all, is what one comes to college for. It would doubtless have displeased his parents if they knew that he was wasting valuable opportunities, which come but once, over a little freshman who was no relative of the Lawrences.

He poled very hard and was conditioned in nothing. So hard did he work, indeed, that when the long, nervous strain was over there was very little stuff left in him. At the senior dance, which came on the evening after the last examination, he ran three girls' cards, and tried to make each think that she was the only reason he had come. This has been tried before. The next day he felt a slight touch of the old trouble.

He became alarmed about himself, felt his pulse, and decided that he needed a rest. He spent three days and ten of his new term cuts at Lakewood. The One of the three girls was there spending Lent.

When he came back to the campus he bumped against that freshman by the lamp-post in front of South Reunion. He was walking with a sportive young class-mate named Thompson, who was a typical little fool, and Darnell said "Hello, Lawrence!" in a tone which just missed being fresh, and seemed to mean "See, I'm not such a poler as you thought." For five minutes Lawrence forgot there was a place called Lakewood, where tall pines murmur.

That evening he heard things about his freshman that he did not want to hear. They were not very bad, but quite enough so to make Lawrence look up his address in the catalogue. He didn't know how to talk to freshmen. They nearly all looked alike. But he rang the door-bell.

It was Saturday evening and Darnell was not in. Lawrence frowned and held that freshmen had no business leaving their studies at night. He shook his head and went back to Jim Linton's room. The freshman had not returned when he called again at eleven.

Lawrence now thought that he had a right to be indignant. He had left a comfortable room, a game of whist, and three class-mates, who gave him many abusive epithets for it, all to talk to this freshman. And see how he was treated! Besides, it wasn't as if Lawrence wanted anything of him. What pleasure was it to him to talk to a little ass freshman? But he was doing his duty anyway.

It did not discourage him. He was not that sort of a fellow. He only shook his head and arose early the next morning, which was Sunday. He hurried through breakfast without stopping to read the papers, and marched straight to the freshman's room on the way to morning service.

Darnell was in bed with a throbbing brow and a slight attack of remorse. Lawrence sat down on a trunk which would have held the freshman's clothes if he had taken them off, and cut a good sermon by the dean in order to give himself the chance of preaching one himself.

"Of course it is not strictly any of my business, but I think you are making a big mistake.

"You must know that it is no great pleasure for me to go out of my way to call a man a fool. But you see I have been through all this myself and I know very nearly all there is to know about it. I have been a great fool in college, and if I can do anything that will prevent another from making the mistakes I made, I ought to go ahead and risk hurting his feelings. Oughtn't I? There's nothing hypocritical in that. Is there?

"This thing of wild oats, Darnell, is all wrong, all nonsense, all Tommy-rot. You know that as well as I do. Of course many people say— But those that say such things are either brutes with no finer sensibilities, or else they are liars, or else they never had any wild oats. They don't know what they're talking about.

"Now, of course, I'm only a very young man, after all. Older men, many of them, would laugh and call me a young prig, I suppose. But I know what I'm talking about as regards myself, Darnell. I know the things I have to think about and cannot forget. I know the things that come up and stare me in the face and make me ache. I know— But never mind all that.

"This is what I want to ask of you: Tell me—you've had your little taste of it now, the glamour is rubbed off, you find there is not quite so much in it as you thought—tell me honestly, my boy, do you believe it pays? Don't you think that one morning like this, with a head such as you have now, and the thoughts inside of it, with a sight of those photographs over there on the bureau, is enough to counterbalance all the fun there is in a month of last nights?"

To this long speech the freshman made no reply, because Lawrence did not say a word of it aloud. In fact most of those grand-stand remarks were not thought out until late that night in bed, while rolling over trying to get to sleep. He would not have voiced them to the freshman anyway. Of course not.

It certainly was "not strictly his business" to walk into the room of a nodding acquaintance and call him a fool in long sentences. Lawrence knew that. And it would have been even worse taste to open up his own bosom and drag out his own private worries and dangle them before the eyes of another. It is only in certain short stories that such absurdities are performed by reserved young men. Lawrence was not that kind of a fool.

The Sunday morning conversation ran something like this, while Lawrence tied and untied the freshman's four-in-hand neck-tie about the foot-post of the bed:

"The Fifty-seventh Street Harrisons? Yes, very well. Were they down there?... Is that so?—to Clint Van Brunt? But I don't like her so well as her sister. Grace is a smooth dancer though.... At Sherry's last winter...." And similar nonsense until the conversation swung round to the prospects of the baseball team, which had recently begun practice in the cage. Then they both woke up and said something.

And throughout it all the freshman was wondering why the mighty senior honored him with a visit, and longing for a drink of very cold water.

Lawrence told himself that this call was merely to break the ice. You couldn't expect him to talk about such serious things when they were hardly acquainted. Could you?

He went again within a few days. He thought he ought to strike while the iron was hot. It was in the evening this time, and the freshman was brighter and better looking. Lawrence liked him more than ever, only he wished that he would not be quite so deferential toward him. Also he greatly wished that he would not consider it necessary to tack those superfluous words to his remarks. It bothered him. They seemed to come out of the refined mouth side wise. Sometimes they stuck, as it were, and hung there while Lawrence shivered. And the more obvious Lawrence made it that he did not consider such emphasis essential to his own observations, the more frequently did Darnell drag it in. This was to show the senior that he need not refrain on his account.

This time Lawrence remained until midnight. They did not once mention the people they both knew in town. They talked about tramping in the Harz Mountains.

It was evident on his third visit that the freshman considered Lawrence's frequent coming due to approval of his development. He stuck it on worse than ever. Lawrence was discouraged and looked it.

The freshman, wondering why his senior friend was so silent, suddenly lifted his big brown eyes. Lawrence was gazing mournfully at him. Naturally this made him feel queer. He became rattled and blushed. Lawrence became rattled and nearly did; and then arose, left abruptly, and kicked himself all the way up Nassau Street, and all along the stone walk past the dean's house, by Old North, in front of Reunion, and into West, where he sneaked up to bed. He did not call again for a month.

Meanwhile the freshman was doubtless running as fast as his legs could carry him, with Thompson and others of that ilk, to the devil. And H. L. Lawrence, Ninety Blank, who by wicked example had started him going, was doing nothing to stop him. Which was the very best thing he could have done.

For this is a sort of a disease, and if it's there it's bound to manifest itself, like other things that break out at about this age. Any fatherly, well-meaning interference, such as a fellow like Lawrence might offer, would have had directly the opposite of the desired effect. If you do not believe this, it clearly indicates that you do not understand it.

Lawrence did not. He, poor devil, skulked off and tried to forget about the freshman, like a rejected lover, and, again like one, he could not, even though he went across the street to avoid meeting those big eyes.

Once more he took a long breath and sneaked off to the freshman's room with a brave lot of kind, smiling advice which he practised saying on the way over. In a moment he came running back to the campus, shouting for joy. The freshman was not at home.

He yelled "Yea" with all his might and danced three times about the cannon, all alone, like a man back on the campus in midsummer. Then because it was Princeton someone else yelled "Yea-a!" from over by Clio Hall. Then Jack Stehman raised his window and yelled "Cork up!" because he felt like it. Someone in East yeaed back in a shrill voice. Tommy Tucker stepped out upon his balcony in Reunion and echoed it mightily. Someone blew a horn, a big Thanksgiving game horn. Others took it up. Windows were thrown open all over the campus. Many voices sounded the ancient cry of "Fresh fire! Heads out!" Shotguns banged. Fire-crackers exploded. Bugles sounded. Distant Dod took up the echo. Witherspoon Hall was already doing its part.

Within two minutes Lawrence was joined by a score of fellows who danced with him about the cannon, yelled "Fresh fier-r-r! Heads out!" until they had brought everyone out they could, then called "Leg pull. All over!" and ran back to their rooms again, feeling that they had done their duty. Windows slammed shut again. A voice from down in Edwards Hall answered "All over!" Every one went on where he left off. All felt refreshed and strengthened for their duties, and Lawrence leaned alone against the cannon. But he too felt better.

He decided that this was a species of Providential interposition, a sort of vision as it were, the interpretation of which was that any man who would allow a little fool freshman to destroy the happiness of the culminating year of the best period of life in the dearest spot on earth would be an unmitigated ass.

He now fell to distracting his mind with work and other things, and realized the beauty of existence, as all undergraduates should. Besides the beauty of existence there were others that he was in the habit of dwelling upon during sunset rambles through the woods down toward the canal; pretty little foolish thoughts which young men who are still students and have yet to choose an occupation have no business in thinking. But the way her hair swept back from that brow of hers on either side of the chaste part and then swirled— But that will do. Lawrence and his affairs already occupy too much space.

And as suddenly as they were interrupted in that paragraph were his walking-time thoughts cut short whenever that confounded freshman loomed up with an arm about the Thompson boy, followed by a brindle bull-dog and a trail of cigarette-smoke.

II

Gussie Thompson was an angel-faced child with pretty ringlety hair, and he had come to college from a strict boarding-school with the intention of making a bad man of himself. And when a boy wants badly to go to the devil there is no reason why he should find it very difficult. In this thought I find I have been anticipated by Virgil.

But though the descent is easy it does not follow that it is always graceful. Thompson, who was conscientiously trying to do it properly, had his discouragements and sour balls just as often as the poler who sat in the next seat and wore trousers that were too short.

People persistently considered Gussie disgustingly good, when in reality he was very bad and smoked big black cigars with red and gilt bands about them. And indeed it is discouraging to walk down to the football practice with the gang, breathing cigarette-smoke at every fifth step, and then have some class-mate you have nothing to do with ask you, before all the fellows, to lead class prayer-meeting the next Sunday. But all that was over long ago.

He now wore the dark bad expression without any conscious effort. No one asked him where the Greek lesson was any more. He seldom had to blow his breath in fellows' faces. And at the club he was no longer obliged to blink and say, "How do I look this morning?" they asked of their own accord, "Full last night, Gus?" just as some people say "Good-morning."

One evening, at about the beginning of the season known to some as "bock beer time," he was in his room surrounded with a few of his own sort, and a knock came at the door. But it was not a very loud one, so he did not take the trouble to answer until there came a second knock, an emphatic one. Then he emptied a lungful of cigarette-smoke and shouted, "Come in and shut your damn racket." He looked up.

Lawrence was framed in the door-way, Lawrence the senior, with his 'varsity sweater and his impressive air.

On the campus Lawrence generally nodded to Thompson, when he remembered him. Once, not long ago, he had walked up the rear stairs of Dickinson with him and said, "What do you fellows have at this hour?" and Gussie wondered when the clubs held their first elections.

With his words of apology and welcome Thompson felt a wave of satisfaction at having a gang about the table with cards and beer-mugs on it. He was glad he had strung the champagne-corks over the mantel-piece.

All of the gang had arisen, and yet this was a Princeton room. If the senior observed the unusual mark he showed little gratitude, for without seeming to be aware of their presence he said, in his gruff voice, "When will you be at leisure, Thompson?" and looked at his watch.

He was the sort of senior that could do these things, and it had the desired effect. They all remembered that they had engagements and picked up their caps and said, "So long, old man," and got out. This was not done constrainedly but as a perfectly natural thing. And Gussie beamed.

The door slammed and the freshman said, "Have a drink, Lawrence."

The senior said, "No, I thank you," and then contradicted himself, "Yes, I will take a little of that." He did not approve of little boys having whiskey in their rooms and big cut-glass decanters on their bookcases, but he remembered something. "That's good whiskey, Thompson." Lawrence sipped and whiffed and held his glass to the light, "excellent whiskey." He gravely smacked his lips. "It reminds me of some Bourbon they once gave us down in Kentucky, on the Glee Club trip—in Louisville, I think it was. They called it Pendennis Club."

Thompson pushed a cigarette-case across the table. "That's Pendennis Club," he replied, simply. "A friend of mine down there sends it to me. I find you can't get good liquor in our part of the country. It's all rot-gut." He twisted his pretty brows into a scowl and emptied his small lungs of smoke aimed at the ceiling.

"I see," said Lawrence, looking interested.

"You know what they say about Kentucky," the freshman proceeded, "for good whiskey, fast horses, and pretty women."

"Yes," said Lawrence.

The freshman refilled his guest's glass with Pendennis Club and his own lungs with cigarette-smoke, which he allowed to seek the free air of the room slowly, with his head tipped back and a mouth twisted scornfully as he had once seen another devil of a fellow do it, who said, "I don't give a damn for the girl." All of which was lost on Lawrence, who was rubbing his chin and looking in the other direction and wishing he had not come.

"By the way, Thompson, speaking of horses, how did you come out playing the races last fall? I often saw you on the train going up—" this was a lie—"when I was slaving over football. Luck stay by you?"

Then the freshman leaned back and said things about Futurity Stakes and plunging at Morris Park and a lucky sixteen-to-one shot, intermingled with a brave lot of profanity and considerable cigarette smoke. Lawrence wore the look of a man listening, and thought up what to say next.

"By the way, Thompson," only it was not by the way to anything but his own thoughts, "where's your friend Darnell? I didn't see him with the others in here."

"No," said the devil of a fellow, "he won't own up to it, but he's a good bit of a poler at heart, Lawrence."

"I did not think it of him," said Lawrence, sincerely. "He's a blame nice fellow though, isn't he?"

"Right. He's the best friend I have. He's pretty young and has a lot of things to learn, but he's a mighty nice man. Awfully clever chap, too. Wish I had his brains. I believe he comes from very nice people in New York, doesn't he?"

"Yes. Thompson, you are dead right in saying he's too young."

A beam of pleasure shot across his young host's face, which was seen by Lawrence, who now felt all right, and began to talk.

"He's entirely too young, Thompson, and the deuce of it is that he doesn't realize how very young he is. A fellow like that never does. You know what I mean. And as far as I can see—I think you had the same thing in mind a moment ago—he is about to make a fool of himself unless he is very careful. He's entirely too nice a fellow, Thompson, for anything like that to happen." Lawrence leaned back and put his feet on the table.

"You see," he continued, "Darnell tries to do things that you fellows do, who are more mature, and he doesn't seem to realize that he is only a boy. Now with you and me it is different. We are older and know things and have been around a bit and— You know what I mean. We can do a lot of things and have a good time and be none the worse for it, but as for Darnell, why, he's a kid, Thompson, a mere kid."

Thompson breathed cigarettes and looked judicial.

Lawrence moved his chair around so that he could lean an elbow on the table. He looked at the fire through the glass of liquid in his hand. "Thompson, I'm in a hole. A bad hole, too. I'm going to tell you about it and maybe ask your advice. I don't mind telling you because I know you can keep your mouth shut. I came here this evening for that very purpose.

"You know I know Darnell's people and all that. Well, I know his sister quite well." That happened to be a lie. "And last commencement when she was down here she asked me to look after her brother when he entered in the fall." That happened to be true, though Lawrence had forgotten it. "She's a pretty good friend of mine, and whenever I see her"—he could not have distinguished her from the other little girls in the school up-town— "she always asks me about her brother. And, well, Thompson, a fellow hates to lie to a respectable woman, you know."

"Only a cad will lie to a decent girl," said the other, sympathetically.

"Certainly. Now, Thompson, I'll tell you what I think I'll do. I am going to very frankly ask you to help me out of this hole." Lawrence looked closely at the freshman. Then he went on, talking rapidly now with his eyebrows tucked down and the words coming between his teeth. Thompson had seen him do it before and had practised it in his room alone.

"You can do it or not, just as you please, but you are the only one whom I'd care to ask to do it. You are the only one I'd trust with it. In fact, you are the only one that *could* do it. Thompson, you know yourself that you have more influence over Darnell than any man in the class."

"Oh, I don't know," the freshman feebly protested.

"Well I do. He has as much as told me so. I am going to ask you very frankly to— I don't know what your views are," the senior interrupted himself, "but I believe in having all the fun in the world I can for myself as long as I mind my own business. But I'd just as soon, when I have the chance—" Lawrence looked down at the whiskey which he was gently swishing around in his glass. He made his voice sound as if embarrassed. "Well, dammit, I'm no saint, but you know it says somewhere that saving one soul will wipe out a multitude of sins or something of that sort."

"God knows we have enough of them," said the devil of a fellow, who now hurled the butt of his cigarette at the fire and arose from his seat. He threw back his head and spoke.

"Lawrence, you needn't say any more. I can give you my answer now." He plunged his hands in his pockets and began striding up and down the room and scowled as he strode.

"Lawrence, I am a peculiar man, and I think my own thoughts and lead my own life according to my own ideas. I keep this room here open to everyone who desires to enter. My whiskey and tobacco is anybody's who wants it. And as long as my guests mind their own business my room is theirs. But when certain members of my class, certain milksops and sanctimonious Gospel sharks come up here and tell me that I am doing wrong and tell me what it is my duty to do, I very frankly tell them to go to hell." He looked around the walls at the Saronys and a French print or two as if to call them to witness, then went on:

"Lawrence, I perceived your drift from the start, and at first, I must confess, I was somewhat taken aback, Lawrence, by your approaching me on such a subject."

The one listening with a bland look of attention on his face and his feet on the table considered this rather fresh, but said nothing.

"But only for a moment," the freshman continued, "only for a moment, I assure you. You talked to me like a man to a man, a real man, not a Gospel shark or a poler, but a man who knows things and yet gives a fellow credit for some good impulses. I appreciate your situation exactly. I have been placed in similar ones myself. I know how it is. And I'm glad you came up here to-night. You rushed in where angels would not have dared, and I'm damn glad you did." He stopped walking the floor. "Now I'm not accustomed to this sort of thing, Lawrence, as you must know, and I won't promise much. But I give you my word, I'll do my best for Darnell."

Lawrence took the hand Thompson dramatically held out to him. He restrained another impulse, an ungrateful one, and said, "Thompson, I always thought I understood you better than your own class-mates did." And Gussie blushed.

The senior arose. "Gus,"—he called him Gus—"I appreciate to a nicety the delicacy of your position in this matter. Please don't let it inconvenience you in any way. I shall always be grateful to you for what you have undertaken this evening, and if I can ever be of service to you, please command me." Some of this was sincere. "I have an engagement now. Good-night. No, I thank you, no more to-night. Come up and see me some time, Gus. Good-night."

"Good-night, Harry," said the other. "Wish you would drop up often."

"I know that," thought Lawrence, as he closed the door, "only I wouldn't say 'Harry' very often if I were you."

Left alone, Thompson took a gulp of whiskey straight without wincing very much, stretched out in a big chair and planned how to follow his friend Lawrence's suggestions, wrinkling his brows and looking no doubt very much like the man of the world that he read about as he did so.

Meanwhile Lawrence was saying to himself, "Still, it's all in a good cause," and hurrying along the street with his coat-collar turned up, like a man ashamed of himself.

"This time next year," he was thinking, "I'll be out of college and hustling in the big world which recent graduates are always telling me I know nothing about. I suppose I shall have to get used to boot-licking and getting pulls. That's business. But just at present I don't like the taste." So he hurried up the street for a counter-irritant, while the mood was on him.

A few moments later he was saying, "The fact of the matter is, Darnell, I'm in a pretty bad hole, and I think I'll ask your advice."

"*My* advice?" said Darnell.

"Yes, if you do not object to giving it."

"I think you know what I mean," said the freshman, "don't you?"

"Yes," said Lawrence, "I know what you mean." He also knew he was finding it a different matter talking to this freshman.

"Well, I'll tell you about it anyway," he went on. "Last year, when your friend Gus Thompson's sister was down here for the sophomore reception—what?" The freshman's big eyes were making him nearly blush.

"Why, Gus is an only child, you know. You must mean his cousin."

"Did I say sister? I meant cousin. His cousin, of course—she's a smooth girl, his cousin. Well, his cousin got at me and asked me to look after him when he entered college and see that he poled and all that. Sort of queer thing, wasn't it? But I promised to do it, and you know you hate to lie to a—well, I hate to deceive her about it."

Then Lawrence went on to point out that while he, Darnell, had plenty of fun in life, he kept up in first division at the same time, which was the way to do, whereas that boy Thompson, who seemed rather immature, had two conditions and was in a good way to being dropped; and he, Darnell, had considerable influence over Thompson—oh, yes, he had: Gus had only that evening referred to Darnell as his best friend, and so on. But Lawrence forgot to say damn this time.

When he finished, the freshman turned toward the senior two fine-looking eyes filled with surprise and some other things which caused Lawrence to feel like a hypocrite, which he was.

"Why," replied Darnell, "of course, Lawrence. To be sure I don't know how well I can succeed, but I'll be very glad to try it. And, Lawrence, I think I ought to tell you that I appreciate your trusting me in a thing of this nature, only———"

"Oh, that's all right," said Lawrence, arising.

"Only, Lawrence," continued the freshman, who seemed to have something to say, "why didn't you tell me this was what you wanted long ago? I would have been willing, I think, without your cultivating my acquaintance so long."

"See here," said Lawrence, with his hand on the door-knob, "to be right honest, I never dreamed of asking you to do anything of the sort until this very day. If I cultivated you it was for yourself and because I like you. I never told anyone *that* before. Good-night."

On his way across the campus Lawrence stopped and told an innocent old elm-tree this: "The man that first said '*Similia similibus curantur*' was very much of a fool. I feel more like a fellow cribbing in exams than I did before." Then he kicked the elm and shouted "Hello-o, Billy Nolan, are you up there?" and ran up the stairs to smoke a good-night pipe and talk about senior vacation. He felt better in the morning.

It was one evening about a week after this that young Thompson came running up to Lawrence's room with a scowl on his face, and talked like an important man in a hurry.

"Why, he's dead easy! I'll say, 'Aw, let's get out of here, this beer is rotten.' 'All right,' he'll say, 'let's wander over to the room.' Minute we get there he proposes that we pole the Greek or something. See his idea? He thinks he'll sour me on being quiet, but, ha, ha! I fool him every time—how? Why I just sit down and pole to beat the band until too late for him to join the gang. See? Oh, but he's easy! I have made up my mind to keep that boy from making a fool of himself, and when I make up my mind to a thing, I don't believe in crawling. Besides, poling won't hurt me any."

"Oh, no, Thompson," said Lawrence sympathetically. "I don't see how it can hurt you."

Darnell came in a little later and sat down in the very same chair and had this to say: "Lawrence, Gus Thompson is a queer fellow. You know he doesn't go with the crowd any more, and because *he* is sour and doesn't care to have any good times, he tries to interfere with my enjoyment too. He's always proposing that we stay in the rooms—you know we room together now. I thought I could look after him better in that way— Well, when he kicks on poling I start to join the gang, and then he says 'All right, let's pole.' He must be jealous about me. But that's the way I work him. He's so easy."

"Yes," said Lawrence, "lots of people are."

THE SCRUB QUARTER-BACK

Tommy Wormsey was a meek little boy with an ugly face, mostly covered with court-plaster, and he would rather fall on a football than eat.

When he came trotting out upon the field, the college along the side lines always smiled at the way he tipped his head to one side with his eyes on the ground, as though he was ashamed of himself and of his funny little bumpy body, stuck into a torn suit and stockings which weren't mates and had holes in them. When he skimmed over the ground and dived through the air and brought down a two-hundred-and-something-pound guard, with his knotty little arms barely reaching about the big thighs, it looked very absurd, and when he jumped up again, yelling "3—9—64" in his shrill earnest voice, and ran sniffling back to his place, with his sorrowful face seeming to say, "I know I oughtn't to have let him slide so far, but please don't scold me this time," the crowd laughed uproariously, which hurt his feelings.

But he paid very little attention to anything except the scrub captain's orders and the admonitions of the coaches, to whom he said, "Yes, sir," and "I'll try it that way, sir." He was afraid of them, and looked down at his torn stockings when they spoke to him. Those of the crowd along the ropes who knew everything, as well as the other spectators who only knew a few things, said that Freshman Wormsey had more sand and football instinct than any man on the field. But they did not know what a coward he was at heart.

More than once when a 'varsity guard had broken through and jumped on him, and the scrub halves had fallen on him from the other direction to keep him from being shoved back, and the other 'varsity guard and the centre, who were not light, had thrown themselves upon these, and one of the ends had swung round and jumped on the top of the pile on general principles, Wormsey, at the bottom, said "ouch!" under his breath, if he had any. He weighed 137 pounds stripped.

At night, after the trick practice with checkers at the Athletic Club, he always hurried back to his room, and stacked the pillows and sofa cushions up in the corner of the room, with the black one in the centre, and taking his place on one knee in the opposite corner, socked the ball into the pile. Every time he missed the black one in the centre he called himself names.

Sometimes when he did this he became excited, and sprang forward and knocked down chairs and tables and things. But he paid no attention to that. He only bit his nails and fell to passing again, and kept it up sometimes until eleven o'clock, which was a whole hour later than he had any business to be out of bed.

But there were days when it became tiresome, this constant pound, pound, pound, fall down, get up and pound again, and once in a while there came dark times when he felt that it all didn't pay, which was very unpatriotic thinking; and the next day, when the crowd yelled, "Well tackled, Wormsey!" he wondered how he could have been such a mucker as to think it. But it was rather hard work for a seventeen-year-old boy whose bones weren't knit to play two thirty-minute halves every day as hard as they were doing now, and then practise place kicks and catching punts afterward, besides keeping hold of all the signals and systems and stuff that were drummed into his little head every evening, along with the rest of the second eleven, in the room across the hall from the one where the 'varsity were learning their systems and signals and tricks.

It's all well enough for them. They have their 'varsity sweaters with the big P on them, and have their pictures printed in the papers, and are pointed out and praised and petted and fondled and fussed over like blue-ribboned hunters at the horse show; but for the poor, faithful, unappreciated scrub it's a different story. There's none of the glory, and all work and grind and strain at the top notch of capacity. And nothing at the end of it but thanks and the consciousness of doing one's duty by the college. So about this time, when they were approaching that critical stage in training which is like getting one's second wind in a cross-country run, he used to have some terrible times with himself. If anyone knew what muckerishly cowardly thoughts he had, he was afraid they'd fire him from college.

He was ashamed of himself, but he couldn't help it. He was getting sick of training, sick of getting up at seven o'clock in the morning and hurrying down to breakfast while the alarm clocks were going off in East and West colleges, and the frost was still on the grass. Every day, as soon as the morning recitations were over, no matter what kind of weather, he must jump into the 'bus at the corner of Dickinson Hall, drive down to the grounds, undress and dress again, and hobble out upon the field, and get his poor little body bumped and pounded and kicked and trampled on, and the rest of his personality yelled at by the captain, and scolded by the coachers, who stand alongside in nicely creased trousers, with canes in their hands, and call out, "Line up more quickly, scrub," which is hard to do when one's lungs are breathless, especially when one is a quarter-back, and needs a certain amount of wind to scream out the signals in a loud enough tone to keep from being sworn at. And that's the way they make football stuff.

To-day he let Hartshorn drag him five yards and missed one tackle outright, and he was discouraged. After the line-up, while they were practising him at catching punts, he seemed to have such bad luck holding the ball; and once, in trying for a wild one when he had run over by the cinder track, grunting and straining, and had put up his little arms, only to feel the ball bounce off his chest, he gnashed his teeth so loud and said "Oh, dear!" in such a plaintive whimper, like a child waking from a bad dream, that two pipe-smoking seniors, who were trooping out in the rear of the crowd, smiled audibly and said something about him. He could not hear what it was. He only heard them laugh, and it nearly broke his heart. But all that he could do was to call them things under his breath, and run sniffling back to his place again.

The trouble with the boy was he had worked so hard and worried so much that he was over-trained, and so, naturally, there was not much ginger left in him. And the reason the keen-eyed trainer did not see this and lay him off for a few days was that Wormsey thought it his duty to make up in nerve what he lacked in ginger; and he was too bashful to tell anyone how difficult it was to make himself play hard, and how that he no longer felt springy when he jumped out of bed in the morning, and that he slept all the afternoon after practice, instead of studying, as all football men should.

He went into the field-house the next day, unbuttoning his coat and hating football. He hated the ill-smelling dressing-room. He was sick of training, sick of rare beef and Bass's ale and bandages and rub-downs, and the captain's admonitions and the coacher's scoldings. He thought he would give anything not to be obliged to play that day. He was sore all over, and his ear would be torn open again, and he didn't like having the blood trickle down his neck; it felt so sticky.

It was a hot, lazy, Indian-summer day; and his muscles felt exhausted. He felt as much like exerting them as one feels like studying in spring term directly after dinner, when the seniors are singing on the steps. As he came hobbling out of the field-house he laced his little jacket, and made up his mind that after the practice he would tell the captain that he could not spare the time from his studies to play football, patriotism or no patriotism. This was not necessary, because he was tumbled over in the opening play, and remained upon the ground even after the captain cried "Line up quickly," with his ugly little face doubled up in a knot.

"There goes another back," said the scrub captain, pettishly, snapping his fingers. "Rice, you play quarter; and Richardson, you come play half in Rice's place."

Another sub and William, the negro rubber, picked Wormsey up, the doctor following behind, and turning back to see the play, which had already begun again, for he wanted to see how the new system was working.

As they approached the field-house he saw the two fellows who had laughed at him the day before standing apart down at the end of the field. One of them was tapping his pipe against the heel of his shoe, and saying, "I didn't know that that little devil could be hurt. He always—" But just then the 'varsity full-back made a long "twister" punt, and he interrupted himself with an exclamation about that. It sounded like a reproach to Wormsey, and he began to feel that he had somehow gotten hurt with malice aforethought. And this made him so ashamed that when they reached the field-house the trainer, sponging his face, said, encouragingly: "That's all right, me boy. Don't feel badly. You'll be out again in a couple of weeks. I've been meaning to lay you off for a while, anyway. I'll tell you for why; you're a little stale, Tommy, a little stale."

Every day now Wormsey trudged down to the field on crutches—they had to be sawed off at the bottom first—and watched the practice from a pile of blankets on the side-lines. It was a fine thing, he told himself, to watch the others do all the work while he sat still with four 'varsity sweaters tied about his neck. This was a great snap; he was still on the scrub, was at the training table, and would have his picture taken, would go to the Thanksgiving game free, and yet did not have to get pounded and pummelled.

He was made a good deal of now. The coachers patted him on the back and said "My boy" to him. He had a lot of sympathetic adulation from admiring classmates. Upper-classmen whom he had never seen before, but who somehow knew him, came up and said, "How's the leg, Tommy?" At which he hung his head and sniffled, and said, "Getting along pretty well, thank you," and then grinned, because he didn't know whether they were guying him or not.

In a few days he could walk with a cane, and he put on his football clothes because they were more comfortable. He limped after the teams up and down the field, and squatted down to see how the 'varsity made their openings, and he learned how to tell, by the expression of his legs, on which side the quarter was going to pass the ball, which nobody else in the world could tell. Also, by carelessly daily sauntering into the cage during the preliminary practising, with a guileless smile on his face, he found out the 'varsity signals, which he had no business to find out.

Sometimes he became very much excited during the scrimmages, and once, when Dandridge, the wriggly 'varsity half-back, kept on squirming and gaining after he had been twice downed, Wormsey screamed, as he hopped up and down on one foot, "Oh, grab—grab him! *Please* grab him! Oh! oh!"

so loud that all the field heard it and laughed at him. Then he realized what a fool he had made of himself and kicked himself with his good leg, and limped slowly up the field to study the next play.

But conceited as it was, he really thought that he would have stopped that runner if he had been there. He imagined just how it would feel to have once more the thrill of a clean tackle, sailing through the air, and locking his arms tight, and squeezing hard, and both rolling over and over, while the crowd yelled in the distance. And he thought it would be fine to get out there again, and run his hands through his hair, and call out the signals, and plunge the ball home into the back's stomach, and then pitch forward, and push and strain and sweat and fall down and get up again. He had a firm healthy skin now, and had gone up to the tremendous weight of 138½, which was vulgar obesity.

One windy sunny day when Wormsey was limping friskily up and down the field with his hair blowing about, Stump, the 'varsity quarter, instead of springing up to his place after one of the tandem plays, as he should have done, lay still on the ground, while the college held its breath.

"It's Stump! it's Stump!" they whispered to one another with scared faces. Then they no longer held their breaths. They moaned, and stamped their heels into the frosty ground, and gazed out sadly toward the dear, frowzy head of the man who was being carried to the field-house.

"It's only a wrench," said the doctor. "He'll be out in a few days."

The captain's mouth grew a little more stern, but he only snapped his fingers, and said: "Bristol! No, he's laid off too. Wait a moment, doctor," he called out. "Is Wormsey well enough to play?"

"Wormsey?" said Tommy to himself in little gasps. "Why, I'm Wormsey. What! play with the 'varsity!"

And the doctor's voice came back through the wind, "No, I think not."

"Oh, yes, I am!" yelled the shrill voice, which was heard all up and down both sides of the field, and reached to the Athletic Club; and throwing away his cane, and bending over to let some one pull off two sweaters, Wormsey ran sniffling out on the field.

"See, Jack," he called to the trainer. "I don't limp a bit." But he kept his face turned to one side so that the trainer couldn't see it twitch.

"Come here and I'll give you the signals, Wormsey," said the captain.

"I know them already," said Wormsey, looking ashamed of himself; and he took his place on one knee behind the centre who had so often tumbled upon him.

Then he jumped in and showed everybody what he had been learning during the past ten days. He was in perfect condition now, except for the ankle, which he forgot about. He was quite accurate in his quick method of passing, and he tackled ravenously. Fellows like Wormsey never get soft. "Just watch that boy follow the ball," exclaimed one of the coaches to another. "Too bad he's so light," said the other.

Once when the scrub had the ball they gave the signal for a trick which they had been saving up as a surprise for the 'varsity. Tommy knew that signal. He dashed through the line between tackle and end, he caught the long pass on the fly, and having plenty of wind and a clear field, he made a touch-down unassisted, which made the crowd yell and applaud. Of course it was a great fluke, and Wormsey knew that, but all the same, while the crowd gave a cheer for Tommy Wormsey, and a three-times-three for "the little devil," he grinned for a moment, and puckered up his eyes. But it is not the crowd that chooses the team.

That evening at dinner all the college was talking about the great tear the little freshman had made, and down at the Athletic Club Wormsey overheard one of the coaches say: "When Stump comes out again, it'll make him work to see the freshman putting up a game like that. But of course he can't keep it up. The pace is too fast."

Wormsey bit his nails and had his own opinion about that. But whatever it might have been was never learned, because the next day he was taken off the field for the season. His bad ankle was sprained in the first half, which served him right for disobeying the doctor's order. But he should not have cared. Didn't he play one whole day on the 'varsity?

WHEN GIRLS COME TO PRINCETON

If you would like to see a college campus as it really is, with students walking along with the gait and the manner and the clothes they usually wear, and to hear the old bell ring, the hall and dormitory stairs rattle, the entries echo and the feet scrape along the stone walks as on ordinary occasions, and see the quadrangle become crowded and noisy, then suddenly empty and quiet again, and if you wish to have a view of your brother's room in its average state of order and ornamentation, do not come to Princeton for one of the class dances, or on the day of a big game, when everyone is excited and well dressed, and even the old elms are in an abnormal flutter, but come down in a small party some quiet day in an ordinary week, when there are no extra cars on the small informal train which jolts up from the junction. Tell your brother that you are coming, or his roommate, who will gladly cut a lecture or two and show you about the campus. Then you may see the college world in its normal state, and the undergraduate in his characteristic settings—any number of him with a pipe in his mouth or a song, slouching across the campus with the Princeton gait, wearing something disreputable upon his head, corduroys and sweaters or flannels and cheviots upon his body, and an air of ownership combined with irresponsibility all over. In short, if you prefer to get some idea of college life, and learn, as far as a girl can, why college days are the best of a lifetime, visit Princeton on some day that is not a special occasion. But very likely this is not what you prefer.

Most girls would rather hurry down with a big trunk in a crowded special train, and go to four teas, meet a score of men apiece whom they will never see again, dance all night, and then, in a few minutes, arise looking as fresh as they did on Easter Sunday, and smile good-byes at the depot to the breakfastless young men whom they leave forsaken and sleepy to try to go on where they left off, while they themselves hurry back to town, and to another dance the next night.

A college dance is generally considered very good fun. There is an adventurous zest in journeying to a college, and exploring it, and meeting crowds of people you never saw before, and there is something wild and reckless in being quartered in an odd little boarding-house, or, more delicious still, in some room in University Hall borrowed by your entertainer for the occasion, with the owner's photographs and souvenirs hanging about just as he left them. Then, too, the young men themselves, some of whom you have met or heard of before, try to be very agreeable, and do everything in their power to make you have a good time, if for no other reason, in order that you may see how superior their college is to any other, so that even several-seasoned society girls consider it worth their while to run down to a college dance, and be amused by these fresh-faced young fellows. Some of them have been coming off and on for several generations of college men, and could talk interestingly of your brother in the class of '88 should they be so inclined. They know all about these hops. This is written for you who have yet to attend one.

There are three regular dances each year, and they are given by the three upper classes. One takes place at the close of the mid-year examinations, to usher in the new term. Another is given at a more beautiful time of the year, usually occurring on the eve of some great baseball game. The third one, the most splendid and most jammed, is the sophomores' reception, given on the night before Commencement to the class which graduates the following day.

Each class has a dance committee, who fly around and work hard to make their dance finer than the last one, and generally succeed. They procure a fine patroness list to engrave on their invitations, containing several of the sort of names that appear in connection with Patriarchs' balls and Philadelphia assemblies, together with those of two or three professors' wives, to lend a tone. The committee get hold of the Gymnasium, pull down the bars and draw the trapeze to one side; then have a lot of pink and white cheese-cloth tacked up, hang some athletic trophies over the rafters, string a few hundred incandescent lights here and there, and send to one of the neighboring cities for a smart caterer and a large high-priced orchestra to come for the night. Then they are ready for you.

Before the dance, however, you are taken to a few teas which are given by some of the clubs. You saw the club-houses when you were shown about earlier in the day. Some of them are very handsome, and they are all nice, and the nicest is the one to which your brother belongs, or whoever owns the club-pin you carry home with you. At the teas the rooms are crowded, the air is hot, the flowers are tumbled over, you become hoarse, and in most features it is similar to any tea, except that there are enough men. You will here meet several of those whose names you have on your dance-card, and you may make up your mind whether to remember that fact or not.

After the round of teas there remain but two hours in which to dress. When you have hurried on those things which make up "a dream," "a creation," or "a symphony," whichever it is that you bring, and have had, if you feel like it, a bit of dinner, you are taken, at a little after eight o'clock, to church. The Glee, Banjo, and Mandolin clubs give a very good concert here, and it is a good place to have your escort point out the various men who are fortunate enough to be on your card, and gives you a good opportunity to notice the taste displayed by other girls in their costumes, and feel pleased with your own. There are all sorts of gowns, made of many sorts of materials with interesting names.

When the concert is at last over—much as you enjoyed it, it seemed rather long to you, who were thinking of what was to follow—you are taken to University Hall, which is across the street, or to the Gymnasium, if the dance is to be there, which is a little farther back on the campus, and you are shown to the dressing-room, where those last fluttering finishing touches are put on. Those calm, assured-looking young women who came in ahead of you are a little excited too, as is that laughing girl who was pointed out to you as a flirt.

When you are quite ready, and are pulling and smoothing your gloves while waiting for the chaperon to start your party, you catch a glimpse of something, as the door opens for an instant, which extends from the door all along the dimly lighted passage to the very stairs beyond—something which looks like a great black bank with gleaming white patches here and there. This is made up of young men, whose collars are stiff and straight. When your chaperon stalks forth with a sort of flourish, several members of the black and white bank come forward to meet your party, and the rest make inaudible comments upon your appearance, probably to the effect that you are "smooth." But all that you are sure of is that your escort offers you his arm with a smile and a stiff bow, that you walk nervously up the winding stairs, step into a dazzle of light, where members of the dance committee are running hither and thither with dance-cards and girls, and where patronesses are smiling, bowing, looking stately, holding their fans, and doing whatever patronesses usually do. Then the orchestra plays a promenade, to which a few impatient couples try to waltz, and you begin what you have talked about and thought about and dreamed about for a month.

You notice when you have danced the first one with your brother's roommate, at whose special invitation you came, that as soon as he has taken you to your seat he rushes off like mad. In a moment he comes back again, bearing with him the young man who was pointed out to you at the concert as being down on your card for No. 2. While he is being presented, still another anxious-eyed man runs up and hurriedly snatches off your host. These are men who are "running" girls' cards.

Now, while you and your new acquaintance are waiting for the music to begin, and are amiably agreeing that the concert was good, that the room is warm, that the light effects are pretty, you may steal another glance at your dance-card to make sure of this man's name. It is carefully written in ink on the pretty silk-and-leather-bound card which was handed to you on the way to the concert. All the numbers are filled and three extras. This is the way it was done:

About three weeks ago a young man was sitting in the grand stand one sunny afternoon watching the baseball practice, and wondering whether the nine would beat Harvard, when one of his clubmates came along and asked him for a match. He complied with the request, and said, "Don't mention it." Then the borrower of the match asked if he were going to the dance, and as he admitted his intention of doing so, he was handed a preliminary card which had your name at the top of it. Then, after a little more conversation, he put his name down for No. 2, and handed it back to your host, who thanked him. And again he said, "Don't mention it." That was the man who is about to dance with you. At that time you were unknown to him. The other names were secured in various ways. In the midst of a lecture your card was passed along to some fellow on the end of the row, who, with the same pencil with which he was taking notes on "Post-Kantian Philosophy," secured for himself a *deux-temps* with you. Other men were hailed out in front of Old North when the seniors were singing, or at the club dinner tables, and in the lounging-rooms when they were talking baseball, or when they were at the billiard table and had to walk across the room to where their coats were hanging to see their cards. Perhaps your host took a night off to it, and went out on the campus and yelled "Hello, Billy Wilson!" under Billy Wilson's window to see if he were in before he ran up the stairs to his room and demanded to see his dance-card; and went on thus from entry to entry as if he were out after subscriptions, except that he went to his friends. Sometimes it is not an easy task to fill five or six cards, especially when every one is feeling rather down-hearted over an unfortunate athletic season. Of course if the girl has been down before, and is well known and popular, there is no difficulty of this kind. Probably the next time you come down you won't need a card.

Except for the five dances which he saves out for himself you see very little of your host during the evening, and even then he seems worried and absent-minded. It no doubt piques you a little that the moment the music ceases he leaves you, and, with an expression on his face which reminds you of when "Pigs in Clover" was the rage, darts across the room, bumping into people and begging pardons. The only time he looks comfortable and recalls to your mind last Christmas holidays is when he and you have slipped off to one of those quiet little nooks so bounteously adorned with rugs and hangings, brought for the occasion from some dormitory room, to enjoy two little bits of ice which he has pillaged from the supper-room. Then for a while he seems to forget his cares, and you two have a good old-fashioned chat. You notice a streak of chicken-salad along his silken collar, but that gives you no adequate idea of the muscle and bad language required to secure and bear away those two little dabs of ice and one napkin, any more than his anxious expression indicates the amount of patience and ubiquity required to "run" three girls' cards at a college dance.

All this time you have been going through the several different stages of "a perfectly lovely time." You have shown a lot of young men how well you can dance, and have gotten along very well with all you have met except that once when you asked sweetly, sympathetically, "Won't you be just too glad to be a sophomore next year?" of a very studious and diminutive member of the graduating class. The chat is no longer about the concert, nor is the heat mentioned, though it is terrific, nor the effect of the lights upon the pink and white cheese-cloth, except by those gallants who see fit to say something about its being becoming to certain complexions. And, most gratifying of all, you notice that those who have your name on their cards more than once come the second time without being brought. Indeed, some come again who have not that good fortune, and you pay slight attention to your card after supper, but dance with those who come up and beg for a dance, because you are tender-hearted and hate to displease them. It is a good plan to lose your card now or hide it. Some girls tear up theirs the moment they come, for fear they might make a mistake, and consequently hurt somebody's feelings.

By this time you have gotten your second wind, if you'll pardon the expression. You talk without previously meditating upon what you are about to say; but you know it's all right just as you drift to the strains of the music automatically. Your eyes are wide open and sparkling; your cheeks have a flush which is becoming; you are dimly conscious that your visit at Princeton is a success. And just as you are beginning to wish that all this could last forever you hear a strain of music of which every daughter of a loving home should be fond, and then, for the first time, you notice that the stately patronesses in their bower are opening their eyes very wide and gritting their teeth very hard. Then, having danced that last one furiously, you are dragged off, casting a lingering glance at faded flowers, wilted collars, tired musicians, torn skirts.

When you come from the noisy, laughing dressing-room a moment later, wrapped from head to foot in a great long thing which covers any changes the five hours' exercise might have wrought in your appearance, you are met by your bedraggled escort under the light, where you took his arm before, long ago, on the way to the dance. You can remember how stiff his collar was then and how smooth his hair. Everything, animate and inanimate, looks different now, especially with that ghastly streak of dawn which mingles with the electric light. It makes some of the girls look rather faded and jaded, you think, and some of the men rather rakish, but not even the girls seem to care very much. Every one is too excited to be tired, and too merry to be formal. All the stiffness of your escort's manner has gone with that of his collar. As he offers his arm this time he does not gaze straight ahead of him and murmur something incoherent about hoping that you are going to enjoy this, for he begins singing "It's all over now," to the dank and misty campus trees on the way to University Hall, and you give him permission to smoke a cigarette, and shout good-night down the stairs, and tell him what time to call around in the morning—later on in the morning—for he has made you promise to stay over all of the following day and see a little of the college and campus, and take a stroll in the queer old town.

Then, as the gray dawn creeps in through the dotted Swiss curtains which somebody made for the freshman who owns the room, causing the roses on the bureau to look pale and livid, and while the far-away voices of the dance committee can be heard from back of Witherspoon, where they are having an informal game of baseball in their evening clothes to celebrate the success of their efforts, and the sparrows outside your window begin to twitter as though there had been no dance, you lay your head upon the pillow and tell your roommate what the tall one said who danced the two-step so divinely, and what that funny little fellow with frowsy hair told you, and what were the remarks of the football man with whom you sat out two dances, and how the entertaining man who sang the solo at the concert seemed to like you, and what your brother's roommate told you not to tell.

THE LITTLE TUTOR

At first they thought he was one of the new students, he was such a little fellow and had such a smooth, boyish face. And one of the college men had stopped him on the street, and, in a manner that seemed to indicate that he had some particular reason for desiring the information, asked him abruptly: "What class do you belong to?"

The little tutor had looked up timidly through his large spectacles and answered, in his thin, high voice: "I am not a member of any of the classes. I am to be one of the instructors in the academy."

He had smiled reassuringly, to show that he did not take any offence. But the tall young man did not seem to dream of embarrassment; he only said: "You *are*?" and passed on.

This happened early in September, the day before the term opened, and the little tutor had been busying himself looking about the campus and getting his bearings in the little city. He had never been in the West before, and this seemed very far out West; it was like a foreign country to him. The broad, evenly laid, well-kept streets lined with so many fine lawns, were a matter of great interest and speculation. He thought it queer that when a man could afford to have nearly a whole block of lawn that he should have only a frame house upon it, but some of these frame houses were very large and comfortable and invariably freshly painted, and he liked that. He admired the new and handsome business blocks of fine brick and stone. But what seemed most wonderful to him was the broad, level sweep of the prairie when he walked out into the country. It almost took his breath away.

But it was the campus, as being his future place of work, that occupied most of his attention and curiosity. He walked slowly over it all, examining each building and every feature thoughtfully and with a critical air as one about to buy. There were only about a half-dozen buildings in all, including both the college and academy. It struck him as odd that both institutions should be on the same grounds and apparently of the same importance. The buildings were rather new, and he missed the dignified, patriarchal aspect of the old campus he had been accustomed to. He thought he could never feel any veneration for all this brand-newness as he had toward those old landmarks he loved so well. Indeed, it all seemed small and puny viewed in this light, and he walked about with rather a patronizing air, as he thought with pride of his Alma Mater, and it seemed to him that this institution was favored in obtaining for an instructor a graduate of such a famous old institution—and an honorman, too, he said to himself, with a blush of satisfaction.

Of course, this preparatory school teaching was only temporary with him. Only a preparation for something else, and that but a step to something higher, until he became—but the little tutor never acknowledged just how high his ambition aimed. It was at this point, as he was leaning against a tree, that the young man had come up and asked him what class he belonged to.

But he had not minded that in the least; he knew how boyish-looking he was. It was very natural for them to make such mistakes. A little thing like that would not discourage him. They did not know him; wait a few days, and they would learn who he was.

And he was right. The whole college and academy learned who he was the very next afternoon in chapel. And even the townsfolk soon learned to know him by sight; they thought it odd that such a little fellow should be a professor. By the end of the month the children coming home from school had learned to point out his small figure with the large head, carried with his peculiar, springing strides, and they would say to one another, "There goes the Little Tutor."

But as they watched him walking briskly by, holding his body stiff and straight, they little knew what was going on behind that smile, which was a curious mixture of gravity and good nature.

For some reason or other things had not gone as he had expected, and so far, at least, they were not tending toward the future he had pictured.

He had thought that out there they would appreciate that he came from such a large, famous old institution, and that he had stood so well in his class and all that; but neither the attitude of the faculty, college, nor academy indicated anything of the kind, he thought. And this wasn't all. No one seemed to take any interest in him as an individual. That is, beyond a cold curiosity.

He did not see why no one took the initiative and made friends with him; he could not, being a new-comer. He knew he had never been very popular at college, but he had a few good friends, and nearly every one of his classmates was kind to him. As he looked back on those dear old days, midst those dear old influences, his present surroundings seemed cold, very cold.

And he could not explain this coldness. Surely it could not all be on account of that first mistake. Oh, that terrible first day in chapel. He thought he would never forget it. He remembered sitting up there on the platform, before all the college and academy—for out there the whole faculty come to chapel, and they sit in a semicircle behind the President. He was conscious of many eyes being upon him, and he knew what they were thinking and whispering to each other, "Is that the new tutor?" "What a kid!" And, indeed, as he cast his eyes furtively over the faces before him he discovered even among the preps. many a raw-boned countryman who was his senior in years, and this thought had so rattled him that he took off his glasses—those large owl-eyed things—and began wiping them, as he always did when embarrassed, and then he suddenly reminded himself that this always made him appear more youthful, and so he clapped them on again. He had not felt this peculiar lonely out-of-it feeling for a good many years; no, not since beginning of freshman year, at his first eating club.

But what was that? He had heard his name pronounced. Surely he was not going to be called upon to lead in prayer. Then the whole sentence re-echoed in his confused brain, the distinct clear-cut words of the President, "Horatio B. Stacy, A.B., will be Professor Wilkin's assistant in the academy." If any of the bold, searching eyes had for a moment wandered from him, he knew they had returned again now. He remembered wondering if he jumped enough for them to see him. He remembered how the steam-heater rattled and pounded in the little chapel and the odor of the new paint, as the young President went on with his perfectly enunciated words in his clear and cold voice: "He comes highly recommended from a good Eastern college. I trust he will prove satisfactory. Let us sing number three hundred and sixteenth." The President pronounced sixteenth perfectly. And the organ burst forth with a loud, cruel prelude, and the hymn was sung. The little tutor always remembered number three hundred and sixteen, one bar of which always seemed to sing "satisfactory."

When the long hymn was finished, the President, having pronounced the benediction, stepped down from the platform and started down the centre aisle, followed by an old white-headed professor, and he by the professor on his left. The little tutor sat next, and so, innocently enough, he started down behind them. How was he to know that there was a custom to be observed in this trooping out of chapel, that the order was determined by precedence? Ah, it made him flush when he thought of it, even now. He could remember just how the whole college and academy laughed—they did not titter, but laughed outright—and when he realized the position and hesitated, trembling, half-way down the aisle, and tried to smile, some of them fairly shouted. He could even now see, in his mind, the face of one of the college men next to the aisle as he leaned back and laughed merrily, cruelly, looking squarely into the little tutor's eyes without pretending to control his mirth. The little tutor never remembered how he gained the cool of the outside.

But why was he to be blamed? They should have told him. How was he to know that there was any rule about the matter? At his college the professors never attended chapel; that is, except two or three, who sat in the stalls.

The next morning, with some fear and much hope, he had met his first class. Perhaps his hand shook a little as he held the roll while his pupils came into the room, and his voice trembled, perhaps, as he addressed the class, and he couldn't help blushing—his old failing—when he heard the laugh caused by his mispronouncing a queer name; but he told himself that he had gotten along splendidly when the long day was over, and the future seemed bright once more as he planned his work.

He thought out just what his attitude toward his pupils would be. He was determined that he would not lord it over them, but would win their confidence, become friends with them, get to know them all personally, and invite them around to his rooms some time, perhaps. He even determined upon his policy of discipline, if that should become necessary. He would not, he thought, be sarcastic with them, as one of his professors at college used to; no, because that, he deemed, was taking a mean advantage of the student, who could not, by reason of the relations of master and pupil, answer back; the master had it all on his side. Neither did he think he would affect the indignant attitude; no, because—well, he remembered the fellows' laugh at him when he once tried to be indignant. He would assume a dignified disregard, as the dean used to. That was the best method of maintaining order and attention in a class-room. That would best become Horatio B. Stacy, A.B. He fell asleep that night wondering what his pupils would give him for a nickname.

Now, as the week went by he never had been obliged to exercise his authority. The classes all paid very good attention, better than he had hoped for. But how very different this thing teaching was from what he had supposed!

The little tutor had been there almost a month; he had walked all around the town and about the country; had faithfully attended all his classes, and sometimes he had six hours a day; had gone to chapel every evening at five; had sat, stared at, in the semicircle behind the President, and had trooped out again with his odd gait, and always the *last* one in the procession now. But he had not a single friend in the State, unless it was his landlady with the false hair front.

He remembered thinking at college that the attitude of those dear old professors was rather distant. But that dignified conservatism was nothing like this unconcern, this icy indifference, manifested by these professors and assistants; and he was one of their number remember, too.

He smiled grimly as he recollected how that, when he first came, he had rather expected that some of them might invite him to dine. This he deemed would be proper in view of his position as an assistant, especially as this institution was so small that the faculty was not large enough to be divided into many cliques. And he had even pictured himself enjoying a delightful conversation with that old, white-haired professor whom he had taken such a fancy to, or, perhaps, holding an animated discussion with some of them as to the respective merits of Western and Eastern colleges.

But he could have endured their attitude if only his plans would work in regard to his classes. It was about his pupils that he thought the most. He made a study of each man and each mind and learned what to expect from each: which were good at one kind of work and which at another; which were the bright, indolent fellows and which were the plodders. They nearly all worked quite hard, that was the one encouraging thing. But he could not understand them. The little tutor had never been to a preparatory school himself, but he felt certain that these fellows were not like most preps. He certainly could not understand their attitude toward himself. He wanted to be friendly with them all, and tried to laugh and joke occasionally to make the relations easy, but it was of no use, they only looked at him inquiringly, as if he were doing something they hadn't bargained for. They all came to recitation in a business-like way, which seemed to say, "Here we are, now you teach us."

They never thought of bowing to him as they came in. They seemed to regard him only as an automaton that was paid—and by *their* money—to stand up there and teach, and he would not have believed that he was thought of by them outside, that he entered into their existence at all, if he had not one day come into the room with rubber over-shoes on his feet and heard them say something about the "Little Tutor." That was the time he learned his nickname, and he felt rather glad when he heard them say it, though they were somewhat confused when they turned and saw him.

When recitations were over, when they had gotten their money's worth, they returned to their lodgings in the same brisk business-like manner, for dormitories are scarce out there. The little tutor thought perhaps this had something to do with the lack of college feeling in the institution. There was no *esprit de corps*. They were, the whole collection of them, college and academy, simply a lot of young men who came together in one place, paid their money and got an education by which they would earn more than enough to repay them. So you see it was a good bargain. Perhaps this was putting it too strongly, he reminded himself, for there was some feeble exhibition of class spirit once or twice, and a football team, too, that practised after supper in their shirt-sleeves. But, oh! how he longed for a sight of those old familiar figures he used to see slouching carelessly across the campus in corduroys and sweaters, with pipes and songs and all that easy good friendship, and the practising at the 'varsity grounds. But these are bitter thoughts.

He hoped that these pupils of his would not always wear linen shirts. He wished their vests were not cut so low. He longed for a sight of a familiar cheviot shirt and a carelessly tied bow at the neck. He would have given a good deal, he thought, just to see one man walking by with a sweater tied by the arms about his neck, a dirty sweater perhaps, and his hands deep down in his pockets. Sometimes he felt that he would enjoy, yes, actually, hearing somebody flunk in one of his classes. Who would have thought that of little poler Stacy?

You see the boy was almost hysterical with this morbid homesickness. He was brim full of it, and a very slight jar would have been enough to upset him and spill it all.

Sometimes he realized that he was making a fool of himself and then he used to take himself in hand for being so childish. But he had always had these little boyish ways of thinking about the people and things around him. He remembered how it was at college; when he first came as a freshman his poor little brain was nearly worn out with wondering and imagining, and when he fell to thinking of those days long ago, it seemed impossible to him that he was a grown man now and teaching in an academy. But it was true, and the framed diploma hung in his room. And, what was more to the point, he was making money. He had felt encouraged when he received his first earnings.

On a Saturday evening he had called around at the treasurer's office and received his money, carefully counted and put in an envelope with a blue lining. The treasurer was an old man with a hard face, and when the little tutor came in he did not say "How do you do," or anything, but simply turned toward the safe and took out the money, keeping the pen in his teeth as he did so, and only taking it out to ask, as he looked up at the little tutor, "That is right," in an exact tone, "is it not?"

He hated this proceeding, and hoped that next time there would not be the right amount, so that he might have a cheque. But he felt light-hearted when he carried the money to his room and wrote his letter home and enclosed a certain share of his profits. Prospects seemed brighter and his hopes ran high, and his dreams ran away out into the future when all his drudgery would be over and he would be recognized as a great man, an authority on—but somehow it was hard to hold those old aspirations that had seemed so realizable about commencement time, when he was an honor man. This cold western climate and these common-sense practical New Englanders seemed to have a chilling effect upon his ambitions, especially as his self-confidence was never very firmly rooted, for he was not, strangely enough for a young man, very much of a believer in himself, and his conceit was not spontaneous, but was of the bolstered-up kind, so that when he halted in his castle-building he was in a very dangerous position, for, if you take a young man's conceit away from him, is he *not* in a very dangerous position indeed?

He was also, he told himself, learning this life lesson: that to win what men call success in this world required something that he was afraid he did not possess: he did not know exactly what to call it. When he was in college he used to comfort himself with saying: "Never mind, you may not amount to much here, but when you get out in the world individual worth will not be handicapped by modesty." But he was beginning to despair of this. It would do well enough in books, but it took what they call *bluff* to get along with men, even if you want to do them good, and this, he knew very well, he did not, and never could, possess. And when he followed this line of thought, he used to sigh and come to the conclusion that what the world called success was not worth the struggle when one had to use such manœuvring to win it. But he reminded himself that he must not allow himself to sink into such pessimism, as in his case those at home had a claim upon him.

It was not at all characteristic of the "little Stacy" of college days to become so despondent, for he was of a hopeful, trusting disposition, and it was all because he had no friend to talk to, no kindred spirit for his confiding nature, or any other kind for that matter.

His discouragement took the form of indignation in the end, but not before he had several times taken hope and smiled in his old trustful way, only to find that it was a blind lead.

For instance when that young Wheaton in his rhetoric class appeared to be striking up a friendship with him, and even walked through the campus several times with him, the chances of having a friend had seemed fair and he began to think that at last he was being appreciated by one fellow, and a nice fellow too. But after young Wheaton had obtained an extension of time on the essay he was to write his manifestations of friendliness suddenly ceased. And the little tutor wondered how he had offended his pupil.

Then there was the time he was invited to a certain annual reception that is always given. The little tutor knew that he was asked only by reason of his position, but he remembered accepting with a good deal of pleasure, and the anticipation of his *entrée* into the society of the town was a matter of no small excitement to him: a good deal depended on it, he had told himself. He meditated considerably over the manner of conducting himself in his first appearance in society as an instructor: what was becoming to a tutor, and just how dignified he ought to appear, and he even found himself practising remarks in his room and examining in the glass the expression of his face and all those old failings of his self-conscious nature of which he was so ashamed. He remembered how excited he was as he rang the door-bell, and how awkwardly he bowed when he had come down-stairs, and how little the people restrained their curiosity in examining him. He did not mingle with the younger people any more than he could help, for he always hated young ladies, but stayed with a group of women who were talking about Emerson.

These ladies were members of a literary club, which thought itself very literary and tried to be Bostonian; and no doubt it was. Stacy had some very good ideas, and would have been willing to express them, and could have quoted readily from an essay he had once written, but somehow they did not seem to be expecting anything from him except to smile and say, "Yes, certainly," now and then, as those two young assistants were doing, and so he tried to pick up a low-toned conversation with one of them on the edge of the circle. But they made themselves so obnoxious by their air of superiority that he boldly made some allusion to the athletic insignificance on the part of their college in comparison with his own. One of them immediately made some answer which brought in something about Yale (at which the other laughed loudly), and then drew up his brow and looked complacent, as if he had made a splendid shot. The poor little tutor turned on his heel furious, and felt a strange desire to swear, something that he had never done in all his innocent life.

He came to the conclusion that the fault of this whole matter lay not in himself, but in them. This is what he conceived to be the reason: Nearly everyone in the little city, students, faculty and townspeople, were New Englanders by blood or birth. That part of the country, like other sections of the West, happened to have been settled entirely by New Englanders. Perhaps they were not all of the best sort of New England extraction either. At any rate no one knew anything but New England ways of doing things and looking at things, and to the little tutor, whose environments had not been such as to cause him to bow down and worship the Pilgrim fathers, or to think that the sun rose and set on Plymouth Rock, all this was at first a matter of surprise, then of wonder, and finally of hate.

Every day in chapel the President spoke in his cold tones of character moulding, and held up before his hearers Puritan models. On Sundays the little tutor went to the principal church of the place, and a kind of essay that seemed to him nothing but washed-out New Englandism was thrown out to him. The text-books were all those of New England writers; all the manners and customs about the college were copied after New England colleges; the very compositions that he had to correct contained allusions to the Pilgrim Fathers and sturdy New England character and noble Puritan traits until the little tutor began to wish that there never had been a Plymouth Rock. He wondered how everyone else seemed to stand it so well. But they had been brought up on it and never knew anything different, and could not conceive of any one's not thinking as they did and as their fathers did and as their great-grandfathers had done, and pitied (only Stacy doubted if they could pity) any family that did not have a piece of the Mayflower to worship.

The most aggravating feature of it, to the little tutor, was that they were so very self-satisfied about it all, never dreaming that there could be anyone so barbarous as not to envy their New England blood, and it was this attitude that used to make the little tutor indignant and cause him to wish he could be sarcastic, as one of his professors used to be: how he would pitch into them! But the worst of it was that he realized his diminutiveness and his boyishness; so he felt helpless and baffled, and he had to submit to the cold indifference and haughty air of superiority worn by those two young assistants not much older than himself, who graduated from such a miserable little unheard-of college. Stacy thought that if they had gone to his college they would have had some of the conceit taken out of them. He thought he might stand it all as far as he was concerned, but he felt somehow as if they were insulting his college in their treatment of himself, her representative. He blushed to think how poor a representative he was.

It was just at this point in his discouragement that he had an opportunity which he had often longed for. At last he would have a chance to show them what was in him. This would be his final stroke, he told himself, and he staked his all upon it. He was to lead the prayer-meeting. These prayer-meetings were attended by the college, the academy, and even the professors.

Like many excessively shy men, the little tutor was not abashed before a crowd when he appeared in some identity other than his own. At college he had always done well in his orations, because unconsciously he merged his own personality into that of an imaginary orator. So on this occasion he was perfectly cool; indeed, he was surprised at himself. The subject was, "Help one another." He had thought, in preparing it, that it was a singular coincidence, his having that subject. He thought he could talk to them from his heart on such a subject. And he did.

They all listened intently, and he thought they must be surprised to see how thoughtful he was, and how earnest, and what a splendid speaker he was. When he finished, he knew that he had done well.

He felt almost joyful when he returned to his room. He dreamed that night that certain men came up to him as he was walking alone, and tried to become intimate with him, as he had seen it done at college with fellows who had suddenly become prominent.

The next morning he was joined on the way to the campus by the principal of the academy. Stacy thought he was going to compliment him upon his admirable talk. But he was mistaken. He even hinted about it indirectly, though ashamed of himself for so doing; but this had no effect. At last, in desperation, he was going to say, "Professor Thorne, may I ask you whether my talk last evening met your approval," but while he was trying to invent some excuse for such a question they reached the academy building.

As he took his seat on the platform waiting for morning prayers to begin (the academy had prayers as well as evening chapel), he looked around at the preps. and studied their faces carefully.

Professor Thorne that morning spoke on one aspect of character-moulding, namely, "Independence." He did not directly mention the address of the evening before, but Stacy thought he might just as well have, as he sat there beside the principal before the eyes of the whole academy without changing his gaze from the floor or moving a muscle, except once, when the principal made some reference to the sturdy New England character; then the little tutor made a slight involuntary gesture, but no one noticed it.

That morning in the class-room the little tutor did not seem himself, and his pupils watched him curiously. And if the conduct and appearance of the little tutor was unusual that morning, what was it in the afternoon!

At one o'clock, when nearly every one went down to get the mail, the little tutor was casually noticed by some of them in the post-office. "Anything for Horatio B. Stacy?" he asked at the window in a high voice. Then they noticed him excitedly tear open the one letter he had received and, as he ran over the contents, he said excitedly, in a voice loud enough to be heard, "Just in time—just," but at that point he seemed to notice that he was being observed. His dazed expression was a curious mixture of surprise and, perhaps, pleasure.

Then he came in late to his recitation at three o'clock and seemed to be barely able to keep his attention on the work, and now and then he would look up and smile and stare at them in an indescribably queer way. And in the midst of the next recitation he suddenly arose and, motioning the young man that was reciting to take his seat, he said, in a husky voice, "Here, stop! the class will please excuse me," and bowing politely, even grandly, he hurried out of the room, not seeming to care that his pupils had not got their money's worth. The little tutor was not himself.

At half-past seven o'clock that evening he came promptly to the faculty meeting and quietly took his customary seat by the door. None of the faculty were aware of anything unusual until after they had transacted the ordinary business and had decided one or two cases that came up, and the president had arisen, as usual, and said, in his clear tones, "Gentlemen of the faculty, is there further business of any nature to come before this meeting?" and the white-headed old professor as usual had turned his head sedately around to see if there was anything, and then settled down in his chair again with his disappointed look, as was his custom. At this point the little tutor arose.

No one saw him at first, and the president was beginning to say "Then the meeting stands adjourned," but before he reached the last word the little tutor cleared his throat with a loud, forced sound, which made them all, young and old, turn their eyes upon him. He was smiling, they thought.

"I think it is about time for me to speak," he said, in his high voice, with a little nervous tremor in it.

He was vaguely conscious of this, and, also, of the light of the lamp reflected upon the blackboard back of the President's head. Then he buttoned up his little cut-away coat and began the speech he had practised in his room. He spoke slowly and, apparently, very coolly, and in a deep voice which he always assumed in delivering his orations.

"You are probably aware, as I am, that in the wording of the letter by which I was engaged to serve as Professor Wilkins's assistant in your academy, there was no clause which specifies the length of time for which I was to serve in that capacity. This is the case, is it not? A purely temporary arrangement, so that, in case I proved unsatisfactory"—he tried to imitate the President's pronunciation of this word—"I need not be retained the entire year.

"I have been here one month," he said, with impressiveness. He paused a moment, and then assuming a smile which he thought was like one of his old classmates, he concluded: "I appreciate the delicacy of your position, and will relieve you of the disagreeable duty—a duty from which you have been restrained by your very kind and thoughtful appreciation for my feelings—by voluntarily offering my resignation."

The little tutor walked bravely over to the desk and bowing low laid a carefully written sheet of paper on the desk, thereby purposely allowing an opportunity for expression of opinion. But he had crossed the room and reached his place before anyone began to speak; at first it seemed as if nothing was going to be said on their part. Then the President at last made answer, speaking very deliberately, it seemed to Stacy:

"Well, Mr. Stacy, this is very sudden; very unexpected. We are surprised. Believe me, Mr. Stacy, in case the performance of your duties had not been satisfactory, we would have advised you."

The little tutor believed him.

"Furthermore, your work has been entirely satisfactory, has it not, Professor Thorne?"

"Entirely," echoed Professor Thorne, across the room.

The little tutor was baffled by the tones of the President. He thought they belied his words. Nobody seemed to be impressed as he had expected.

"It is my intention to leave to-morrow!" he exclaimed, excitedly, making an emphatic gesture with his hand.

"Surely, Mr. Stacy, you are laboring under some wrong impression. Surely, there is some misunderstanding. You are a little excited, Mr. Stacy. Perhaps you are a little overworked. You had better think it over before you make up your mind permanently."

Professor Thorne here spoke up: "Don't you think, Mr. Stacy, that it would be a little unwise on your own account. Pardon me, Mr. Stacy, but I understand your circumstances, and it would be rather late in the year to obtain another position now."

The President was about to say something further, but as he turned he saw on the young man's face a look as of a weak animal at bay; and he stopped.

"Don't you know why I'm leaving this place? I'll tell you," he exclaimed, excitedly; all his oratorical manner and assumed grandiloquence was forgotten with the rest of his speech. He almost screamed in his natural voice, "I'll tell you, I HATE you—all, every one." He swept his hand wildly around the circle, "From the oldest, gray-haired D.D. to those two conceited young assistants, you cold, intellectual, cultured, bloodless, unemotional, self-satisfied creatures—I HATE YOU. Of course *you* don't care; you won't lose anything by my hate." He paused a moment, buttoned up his little coat and began again, the words pouring out of themselves: "I know I'm nobody; I know I'm not attractive, or cultured, but I'm a human being—if I'm not from New England—and I have a human heart. I have been here a whole month, and in that time what one of you has made a friendly advance?—has spoken a word of encouragement?—has even taken note of my existence, except as a machine paid to do a certain amount of work? I found that out that first day in chapel when your President told you all of the bargain he had made. He assured you that you were not cheated, as the article rented had had a good standing in his class. I wondered at the time he did not, in naming my good points like a horse, mention my college instead of saying *a good Eastern college*—that's what I can't stand. I could endure the treatment of myself, but those slurs on my college I cannot and will not stand. Stop! Don't get excited; don't try to explain anything. You don't want me to go, because you think you have a good, hard-working horse. You think to detain me by informing me of my poverty. That might do, but—but read that!" He snatched from his pocket the letter he had received that morning.

"*Read that!*' and he started toward the desk with the letter in his hand. But the strain was too much for the little tutor. He fainted for the first time in his life.

He never found out whether they read the letter or not. Of course, he could have ascertained by writing out there, but he never did. Indeed, he did not like to think of that time now, though he did love to take out a certain letter with a printed head at the top and read the formal language which stated briefly how that, owing to the fact that Mr. Charles Benjamin Howard had decided, etc., "the fellowship in, etc., was open to Horatio B. Stacy as being, etc., and that it was with a great deal of pleasure"—but he knew it all by heart, because he had intended to repeat it once on a certain awful occasion when he was, he thought, temporarily insane, at least not Horatio B. Stacy.

COLLEGE MEN

"Johnnie, Johnnie, Dagnan,

Johnnie, Johnnie, Dagnan,

Do you want me?

No, sir-r-ee,

Not this afternoon, 'ternoon, 'ternoon, 'ternoon."

That is what a crowd of noisy, lazy, slouchy-looking fellows, in a circle in front of Reunion were singing to a little, old, dried-up man, with a plaintive face and blue uniform, in the centre of it.

John Dagnan, chief of college police and envoy extraordinary to the faculty, cast a sad reproachful glance at two of the number to whom he had borne many a summons to appear at one o'clock, and then relapsed into his characteristic melancholy silence, gazing inscrutably into the distance.

Over by the elm in front of the *Princetonian* Office were four seniors pitching pennies and looking very much in earnest over it. Up and down in front of the shambling old building two or three base-balls were flying back and forth over or against the heads of the loafers and passers-by. Several other groups were merely sitting on the steps or standing on the stone walks, talking or whistling or waiting for nothing.

The steps in front of the entry door were so crowded that young Symington, following his friend Tucker, had to tread upon some of the loungers to get inside. But the loungers were used to that and did not stop their conversation. It's easier than arising.

Symington would have liked to stop and watch the fellows pitching pennies, and hear more of the song, and see what the little policeman was going to do about it, but he did not say a word. He merely followed Tucker up to his room and wondered why he failed to notice it.

Charlie Symington was a well-built prep. boy who had been known to strike out three men with the bases full. He had been invited to spend Sunday in Princeton by some important athletic men in order that he might see how much better their college was than all others in the world. This was because Charles was young and foolish and had shown signs of shifting his youthful affections and his future athletic brilliance to that other college where two of his intimate friends were going, and which had brilliance enough already.

These athletic officials thought that this would be narrow-minded in him, and they were giving him a very good time. The way they did it was not by treating him as a distinguished guest or by telling him what a fine fellow he was, which would have turned the little boy's head and have made him think he could do as he pleased. They simply said "Come," and when he came, let him walk around with them.

For they were a right conceited lot in regard to their college, and thought that all they had to do was put a boy on the campus, let him use his eyes and breathe the air and get it in his young system, and his good sense would do the rest. If it did not, his sense was not good and they did not want him, thought they.

As for the young pitcher, he did not quite understand why these great and awful men whom he had often heard of were so kind to him, and he did not care. He only opened his eyes and ears and shut his mouth, and let his friends do whatever they wanted with him and thought it was very nice in them.

And that is all I am going to tell of; what Symington the prep. drank in with his eyes and ears open and his mouth closed. Nothing will happen.

A lame arm had laid him off his team for the usual Saturday game, so he had arrived in Princeton this afternoon in time to see the 'varsity play with a small college nine. He watched the game critically and closely, and passed judgment on each player—under his breath.

He knew the initials, age, class, and previous history of every man on the team, and he could have told you just what each one did and did not in the seventh inning of the Yale game two years before. In regard to the important games previous to that he was somewhat hazy. He was only sure of the scores by innings, the total base hits, and the errors, though he hated to confess it.

Tucker, the Base-ball president, had honored him to the extent of allowing him to sit on the bench under the canopy with the team. Here was a splendid opportunity of gazing upon their faces at close range. Once when the third baseman came in breathless from a home run, with perspiration running down his face, he tripped on Symington's toe and said to him in a loud tone, in order to be heard above the applause, "Pardon me, Symington," which Charlie did.

After the game, which was of the subdued, half-holiday recreation sort, good to bring either a pipe or a girl to, without fear of putting either out by inattention, Tucker, the president, brought him up the street and through the noisy quadrangle to Reunion Hall where he now was ascending the stairs.

Tucker opened the door and picked up a dozen or more letters from the floor and said, "Sit down, Charlie," and began to assort them.

But he said "Sit down Charlie" in an absent-minded tone, and Charlie knew that, and so he looked about the room instead. He thought this was the kind of a room a college man ought to have. He gazed at everything in it from the oar of the last Princeton crew (which must have rowed in triremes—there are two hundred and nine of those oars) to the small photograph of a girl's face in a dainty little figured blue silk frame, all alone over Tucker's desk. That was the first thing he had discovered of which he could not approve. It grieved him to be obliged to think that of Tucker. He seemed such a fine fellow, too.

Just then Mercer, the treasurer, came in with his rattling tin-box, and talked business with Tucker, who nodded his head and kept on opening and glancing through letters.

Symington tried not to listen, but he couldn't help hearing, so he got up again and went to the window. A great lot of racket was going on in the quadrangle below. Somebody had thrown some water out of a window at somebody else, and now they were trying to throw stones back without breaking glass, which was hard to do. Everyone was shouting or yelling, or both, and it was echoing from Old North and College Offices. This is called Horse.

It interrupted Tucker so that he had to raise his voice and repeat several times what he said to Mercer. Finally the voices became louder than he liked. Stepping across the room in a matter-of-fact way with an open letter in his other hand, he threw down the window from the top, with a shrill squeak, and said, in a casual tone, "Ah, I'm afraid you'll have to be just a little bit more quiet down there. You're getting a trifle too noisy. There, that's better," and went on with his sentence to Mercer, who answered, "That's so. Shall I wire him about it?" The racket had suddenly subsided.

Symington the prep. sat down and looked at Tucker. But the senior changed his expression no more than when he knocked the ashes out of his pipe. Charles asked no questions because he was not that kind of a prep., but he arose, went to the window again and looked at the horse-players. Then he looked at Tucker once more. Most of them were bigger than Tucker.

They acted as if nothing unusual had taken place. They were laughing now at something else, only it was quiet laughter. They were under-classmen.

The two athletic officers were busy now, the president talking very rapidly and seriously, and the treasurer listening intently. Symington, the prep., gazed out of the window as only preps. can gaze. He found it interesting enough.

It was that hour of the day when the undergraduate leaves whatever has been occupying his attention, and thrusts his hands deep into his pockets, and heads for the spot in town where he feels like going three times every day. There were dozens of them in sight doing it now.

The prep. thought it odd, the way some of them stood still out in the middle of the campus, and with their eyes turned toward an upper story of one of the buildings yelled, "Hello-o, Sam, going down to grub?" or beseechingly, "Please shake it up," or commandingly, "Get a move up there!" He liked it though.

He could hear footsteps rumbling down the entry stairs, then the door slam, and then the man himself would emerge in sight. He saw them coming out of North, too, and from West, and he could make out others, way over by East College. Many of them headed toward Nassau Street. Some set out in the direction of the Chapel. Others turned toward the Gymnasium. Nearly all of them whistled or made a noise of some sort as they went along.

One fellow, a tremendous man, was stalking by with his head thrown back, singing at the top of his voice. But the funny part of it to Symington was that the big fellow's face seemed utterly unconscious of whether any one was around to see him or not. He was all alone, and he seemed to be having a quiet, comfortable time of it.

When the clock tolled six Tucker arose and said, "Now we'll go and get some dinner, Charlie—Pat, Symington and I dine at the Athletic Club this evening. We'll see you later." Pat was Mercer's right name.

Symington was glad to hear that he was to dine at the Athletic Club this evening. He had read all about this affair, and had seen pictures of it in *Harper's Weekly*. But he listened attentively to all Tucker had to say on the way down.

His friend opened the heavy oaken door with a small flat key, explaining that it was necessary to keep the doors locked because the mob would otherwise make themselves at home in there. "You see, Charlie," he said, "although this is the training-quarters it is a private club, and not a public affair like the field-house we were in this afternoon. But the membership is open to every one for competition. When you come to college, if you make the team, you will be a member as long as you are training with it. If you become a captain or get any of the Athletic offices you'll be a life member."

But Symington the prep. was not listening to that. When the door opened he caught a glimpse of a big brick fireplace with tiling over it, on which was inscribed "Oranje Boven," and higher up were footballs hung in clusters with scores painted upon them, and all about the wainscoted walls of the hallway were baseball and football and lacrosse championship banners with gilt lettering. That's what he was paying attention to.

"Yes, leave your cap there, any place. Now I want to see what you're good for in this line. We'll go over the house afterward." Tucker led the way toward the sound of knives and forks.

Now it should be understood that Symington, the head man of the school, was not afraid of anything on earth, and if he were dining at Prospect with the President of the University, it would not have mattered. But to walk straight into a room and be introduced to the captain of the team was a little too much. It took his appetite away at first, and he thought he could eat none of that famous training food of which he had heard. However, the shock soon passed.

He was presented to all the members of the nine, and to the subs and to the trainer, and also to two professional pitchers from the Brooklyn League team, who were down to coach the players, and who were just now eating with their knives a huge meal at a little side-table.

Symington was given a seat next to Jack, the trainer, who was cordial and kind to him, and said, "Oh, me boy, you must eat more than that."

The meal seemed to be a very business-like affair. The men were brown from their exercise in the sun, and ruddy and glowing from their recent rub down, and hungry from both causes, and they devoured great sections of rare beef as though they knew it was their duty to get strong for Old Nassau.

The conversation was quite shoppy. When he had finished, the captain pushed back his chair from the table and said, "Fellows, you played a pretty good game to-day. But we've got to brace up in team work. When a man's on a base we must simply push him the rest of the way around."

As soon as dessert was finished, Tucker said, "I want to smoke. Let's start up for the singing, Charlie."

Symington would have liked to explore the rest of the club-house, though of course he did not say so. He did not even ask what the singing meant. But as they arose to leave the table he did ask a question about one of the portraits of the ancient and modern athletic heroes which line the walls.

"Yes, Charlie," said Tucker, "that's he."

"I remember just how he looked when he made that long, low drive, that time, in the ninth inning," Symington said, solemnly.

"Yes," said Tucker, briefly, "a great many of us will always remember his long, low drives. Here is your cap."

This was in reference to a large portrait at the end of the room. The frame had a deep black border.

Tucker and his friend, the other fellow, the University treasurer, whose name the prep. had forgotten, waited until entirely out of the house before lighting their pipes.

Two or three of the team joined Tucker and Symington and the University treasurer. The prep. felt that one of them was coming up beside him. He waited a moment and then glanced out of the corner of his eye. He caught his breath, but did not fall down. It was the captain of the 'varsity nine.

It's a very fine thing to be head man of your school and pitcher on your team, but oh, if the school could see him now!

"How do you like our club?" asked the captain in a voice something like other men's.

"I like the club," said Symington.

"Yes, we think it's a pretty comfortable place. Come down to-morrow and we'll show you the Trophy-room and all." Then he began to question him about his team at school.

To Symington's surprise and delight the captain seemed to know the score of all the important games they had played and how many—or how few— base hits had been gained in each one off him, Charles Symington. And he can tell you to this day every word of the conversation and at what point of the walk it was when the captain said, "Well, you are pitching pretty good ball this year. This is McCosh walk. Look at those trees."

"Yes," said Symington.

The soft evening light was sifting down through the interlacing branches, making a glow to dream about, which Symington did not notice. He had no time to waste at present.

They passed between Chapel and Murray Hall and across back of West toward North. Just as they reached Old Chapel strange notes of music broke in on the prep.'s ears. At first he could not make up his mind whether it was vocal or instrumental, or whether it was real at all, in fact, or part of a dream like everything else perhaps. The seniors were singing, and from that part of the campus it echoes oddly, as you doubtless know.

When they turned the corner and were on the front campus a wonderful sight met the prep.'s eyes. On the steps of Old North, and spilling over upon the stone walks in front and filling up the window casements on either side, was the senior class in duck trousers and careless attitudes with the dark green of many class-ivies for a background and the mellow brown wall of the ancient pile showing through in places. Most of the fellows had an arm about one or two others.

One of the number was standing up in front beating time with a folded *Princetonian*. They were singing a dear old song called "Annie Lyle." Their voices came rich and sweet in the twilight air.

Under the wide elms were the rest of the college. Also the poor post-graduates and some of the faculty's families and the little muckers, and even a few seminary students from over the way. But only the undergraduates seemed becoming to the scene. The others rather spoiled the effect.

Some of the fellows were sprawled out flat on their backs looking up through the tree-tops at the fading blue. Some rested their heads on each other and got all mixed up so that no one could tell which were his own legs. Others were strolling about or looking at the strangers who came to spend Sunday or to see the game. A few were passing tennis-balls and being cursed by the rest. All of them wore négligé clothes or worse.

The captain said he did not feel like singing and led Symington across in front of the seniors and made him sit down beside him on the grass. This was in the eyes of the whole University.

Symington was quite near the men on the steps. He looked them over and tried to catch the joke they were all laughing at now the song was finished. He thought it would be a right fine thing to sit up there and sing to a college. And he made up his mind that if he ever did it he would climb up on top of one of the lion's heads like that little short fellow with the long pipe.

After singing "Rumski Ho" in long, measured cadence, and other good old things and several new ones, some one on the steps began shouting, "Brown! Brown!" Several voices said, in concert, "We *must* have Brown." Out in the crowd they began crying, "Right! Brown. We want Brown! We *must* have Brown!"

Three seniors lay hold of one senior and lifted him to his feet. Symington could hear him saying, "Don't, don't. I'm a chestnut. They won't listen to me any more. Please don't make a fool of me, fellows." But he was made to stand out in front and sing a solo.

While this was going on the rest of the college jumped up from their places and pressed up into a close semicircle about the steps. Symington and the captain had to arise to keep from being trampled on.

When Brown finished his solo he was applauded so much that he had to sing another, and Symington made up his mind that next to being the captain he would most like to be Brown.

Then the crowd called for "Timber," and a man got up who had the queerest face Symington ever saw. He looked as if he were trying with all his might to look serious and would never succeed. Everyone began to laugh the moment Timberly stood up, especially his own classmates. And when he began to sing his comic ballad they laughed still more.

When he finished, the audience clapped their hands and yelled. A crowd of juniors gave the college cheer and ended with the words "Timberly's Solo." In some respects Symington liked Timberly more than Brown.

When Timberly at last, looking sad, sat down, Symington heard several voices saying "Everybody up." Those on the ground arose, and those in the windows jumped down. Symington got up too, though he did not know why, and took off his cap when he saw the captain do it.

It was late twilight. The campus was becoming dusky. The faces were dim. The ball-throwing had ceased, and the little muckers had left. The elms were sighing softly overhead in a patriarchal sort of way. Symington thought everyone seemed more quiet and solemn than they were before. Perhaps he only imagined it.

Then, with all the seniors on their feet, with their heads uncovered, the leader waved his white baton, and over one hundred voices sang "Tune every heart and every voice, Bid every care withdraw," and the rest of the college hymn.

Many of the audience joined in, and nobody thought it fresh in them; and Symington would have liked to join in too, only he did not know how. He felt very queer for some reason, and forgot who was standing beside him for a moment. The poetry of the scene was getting into him. He didn't know that, of course, but he had a vague feeling that this was living, and that it was good for him to be there.

When the hymn was finished the class cheered for itself and for the college, and for itself again; and the senior singing was over.

From all over the front campus there suddenly broke out in many loud discordant keys, "Hello, Billy Minot" and "Hello, Jimmy Linton" and "hello" Johnnys and Harrys and Reddys and Dicks, and Drunks, and Deans, and Fathers, and Mables and horses and dogs and houses and others. As each found the man he wanted, an arm or two was thrown about a neck or two, and they started off for some other part of the campus or town.

The captain had also helloed for someone. Symington was left alone for a moment. But he was not exactly alone. He listened to the scraps of talk as the fellows moved past. "Pretty good singing this evening.... Get to work now.... At Dohm's.... I told him to come up.... New York to get advertisements.... The Trigonometry.... Trials for the Gun Club.... *Princetonian* Subscriptions now.... The mandolin to some girls that came to see the game with him.... You damn sour ball." Some of them were humming the last notes of the song. Others were saying nothing.

A loud clear voice beside him called "Hello, Charlie Symington." It was Tucker looking for him in the dusk, and he called him just as they called to college men. Symington was to meet the captain again later on. Tucker put his arm about Charlie's shoulders as they stepped along toward Reunion. Perhaps he did it unconsciously.

"You can amuse yourself with these," said Tucker, tossing into Charlie's lap a copy of the *Bric-a-Brac*, which he had read long ago at school, and a lot of photographs. "And if you want a nap," he added "just read that." He threw across the room the last number of the *Nassau Lit*. That's a very old joke.

Tucker then turned to his desk and got to work over something. Symington did not know what it was, and of course did not ask. But it was not fifteen minutes before "Hello-o, Tommy Tucker" came in a loud voice from the quad, below. Tucker frowned and did not look up.

Then it came again, with a sharper accent on the second syllable, "Hell*oo*, Tommy Tucker."

"Hello," Tucker replied, shortly.

"Are you up there?"

"No, I'm down at the 'varsity grounds running around the track."

"You busy?"

"Yes, Ted, I am. Don't come up."

"All right." Then a whistled tune began, and the shuffling of a pair of feet along the walk. Gradually they faded and mingled with other whistling and feet scraping.

While Symington was thinking this over he heard another voice calling for someone else, and when a muffled response came back, the clear, outside voice said, "Stick your head out!" He heard a window lowered and the inside voice say "Well?"

"Stick it in again."

The window slammed and the man below went on down to Dohm's, whistling softly to himself.

Symington, the prep., thought that was very funny and laughed aloud, and hoped he did not disturb his host by so doing.

Presently someone else yelled for Tucker, and when he replied, "Yes, of course, I'm busy," the man below called back, "Too bad," and the entry stairs began to clatter. In a moment a broad smile and a pair of clean duck trousers burst into the room.

"Timberly," said Tucker, smiling in spite of himself, "I thought I told you not to come up here this evening."

"I believe you did. That's so." Timberly was trying to look serious. Then brightening up at the sight of Symington as if remembering something. "But you see," he said, "I wanted to meet the pitcher." Tucker grinned and introduced them.

Timberly shook Symington's hand vigorously and said, "Wasn't that a smooth song I sang on the steps—hey? I'm a good one, only none of 'em appreciate me. Oh, yes, I nearly forgot—I'm up here on business. I'm up here on business, Tommy Tucker," he repeated, and daintily kicked off Tucker's cap and disappeared into one of the bedrooms. Tucker kept on working. Symington wondered what Timberly was doing.

It was nearly half-past eight now, and other fellows began dropping in. Some helloed first and some came unannounced. Tucker looked up to see who they were. Sometimes he said "Hello" and sometimes he did not. Some of them took off their caps. Others did not. Tucker left it to the first ones to introduce Symington to the later ones.

After half an hour's absence Timberly emerged from the room finishing a sentence he had begun before he opened the door. "And Tommy, you must do the rest. You can tie them so nicely too."

"Tommy, look," said the man with the banjo on the sofa.

Timberly was standing up straight, nicely incased in evening clothes and holding two ends of a white tie in his hands. He looked well-groomed and seemed like a different man now. Perhaps he was.

"What are you doing?" said Tucker, in a stern voice.

"I've got to do it. It's two years now, and it's not good form to let a dinner call go more than two years in Princeton. Here, Tommy, fix this."

"Do it yourself."

"These were great friends of my brother's, and he made me promise on the Family Bible, if we have one. Here, tie this. Great Scott, I've done all the rest. They are your own clothes. You ought to at least be willing to fix the tie."

Tucker put his pen between his teeth and tied the knot with Timberly kneeling at his feet like a patient child having his face washed. Tucker was one of the three men in college who could make a decent job of a tie on another man's neck without standing behind him. The others looked on in silence. Timberly looked up and winked at the prep.

As a rule Symington did not like people to wink at him, as though he were a boy, but this was a most peculiar wink. He not only liked it but nearly snorted out with laughter, which would have been a very kiddish thing to do.

Timberly jumped up. "You're a pretty nice fellow, Tommy Tucker, even though you are arrogant," he said, and leaned over and rubbed his chin affectionately across Tucker's nose, then grabbed his cap and started for the door.

"By the way Timber," said Tucker. "I want you to return those clothes some time. Do you hear? I may go out of town next week."

"That sounds reasonable," replied Timberly, reflectively rattling the knob as he glanced about the room at the others.

"And I don't want to chase all over the campus for 'em. Do you hear?"

"Now, Tommy Tucker, you talk as if I were accustomed to keeping things I borrow. What are you fellows laughing at? Besides, you know very well, T. Tucker, that even if I should happen to forget to return your suit, all you would have to do would be to wire down home for mine—or, no, ask me and I'd wire down myself and save you the trouble." He banged the door.

"Now do you suppose," laughed the one with the cigar on the divan as Timberly's feet in Tucker's patent leathers went pattering down the stairs, "that Timber thought he was in earnest in that last brilliant remark of his, or was it meant for horse." You could seldom tell with Timberly.

"I don't believe he knew himself," said the man with his feet on the arms of Symington's chair. "He's on one of his streaks to-day. I saw the symptoms this morning in Ethics. And when he's that way he's as good as crazy."

"Right," said the one with the banjo. "He don't know what he's saying any more than he knows that he has a cap on his head with a dress suit. If he were in his right mind he would not go out calling."

"He'll either make a fool of himself this evening wherever he goes, or else he'll make one of those great tears of his."

But Symington the prep. thought Timberly was about the best fun in the world.

Some of the fellows left and others came in. Symington thought some of them behaved oddly. One man seemed very sour and came in scowling and sat down without saying hello to anybody. He put his feet on the table and pulled his cap down over his eyes. As soon as he finished his pipe and had emptied the ashes on the carpet to keep out the moths he arose and stretched himself and went away again. He had not said a word. And after he had left no one said anything about it.

That happened while the crowd was thickest. When there were only a few fellows in the room some one generally remembered to introduce the incomers to Symington. He rather liked the way they treated him. They did not, as a rule, patronize him because of his being a prep. And they did not take pains to make him feel at ease, which would have rattled him. They treated him more as if he were one of them, and talked to him, if they felt like it, and let him look after himself, if they did not. At least that is the way it seemed to Charlie. And they called him Charlie or Symington, without any Mister, which would have made him feel ridiculous.

And all this time Tucker at his desk kept on working and only looked up occasionally to say, "How are you, Willie, there's the tobacco, come in." The only time he arose from his seat was once when Jack the trainer came in, and looking at the crowd said, "Mister Tucker, can I speak with ye a moment." The busy man said "Certainly" and led the way into his bedroom and closed the door with a bang, and came out again in a few minutes saying, "All right Jack, I appreciate your position. I'll see to it. Good-night," and sat down to work again.

At a little before eleven the prep. began to feel the force of training habits. He was gritting his teeth hard to keep from yawning. Tucker, who had not looked up for nearly an hour, whisked his papers and things to one side, slammed two drawers, turned a lock, and suddenly jumped up from his chair. He ran across the room with a yell which startled the prep. and made the chandelier ring. Then he threw himself upon two fellows on the divan and began calling them names. His teeth were set and his face so fierce that the prep. found it difficult to keep from believing him angry. And then the two on the divan arose in their might and cast him upon the floor, exclaiming, victoriously, "There, be Gosh." Tucker was through his work for the week and was feeling glad about it. That was his way of expressing it.

"Now, Charlie," he said in a loud, careless manner, "we go out and have some fun now. Here's a cap. Don't wear that ugly stiff hat any more. See?"

Symington had no idea where he was going, but he arose and said good-by to the three others in the room. They did not seem to feel badly in the least over their rude treatment on the part of their host. One of them, sitting on a table with one foot on a chair and the other on the floor, was reading a book of verses and did not look up when Tucker said, "So long." The other two, who had been talking about the baseball prospects and including Symington in their conversation, remained flat on their backs talking about the baseball prospects without Symington.

It was a beautiful evening. In other words it was spring term and the night was clear. There were still groups of fellows seated on the doorsteps or stretched out under the trees. The gleam of their flannels could be seen in the dark. They were up in the balconies also. One of them knocked the ashes from his pipe and Symington saw the sparks float down. He heard a low laugh come from one of the wide open windows. Up from Witherspoon came the tinkle of mandolin music. They were playing to some visiting girls on those broad balconies in front.

"This is West," said Tucker; "Jack Stehman lives in that room up there and Harry Lawrence in the one below———"

"Oh, Stehman the tackle?" asked the prep.

"Yes. Have you met him?"

"No."

"You will to-night."

The prep.'s heart gave a bound. He was to meet Stehman.

They passed down by Clio Hall and dingy Edwards and turned toward a long gray building a little to the left.

"This is Dod Hall," Tucker said, and opened one of the big doors.

They went up two or three flights of stairs and turned down the hall, and Tucker kicked a door at the end of it. Something clicked and the door opened of itself. Four or five voices shouted, "Come in."

Mingled bits of conversation and tobacco smoke and the odor of lemon-peel met them in the little hall-way as they entered it. But Symington the prep. looked behind the door and made up his mind that his door would have an electric apparatus like that when he came to college.

A fellow stuck his head out of one of the bedroom doors and pointing across the hall-way to the main room with a long, bright deer-knife, said, "Come in, Tom, I'll be there in a moment." He rubbed perspiration from his brow with the back of the hand which held a lemon and disappeared into the bedroom.

"Yea-a-a!" cried several voices as Tucker pushed back the portière and stood in the door-way. "Come in, Tommy," they said. "Come in, Symington," said one of the fellows that knew the prep.

"Fellows, this is my friend Symington, the prep.'" said Tucker; "Symington, this is de gang." Tucker tossed his cap and Symington's gracefully into the scrap-basket and pushed Charlie into a seat on the sofa. A fellow with spectacles began asking him what he thought of the afternoon's game. The prep. did not know the man's name, but that did not matter.

There were about a dozen fellows scattered about the room, but the thing that attracted Symington's attention was in the centre of it.

Two square-topped desks had been placed end to end. On these lay a table-cloth, or rather some sheets, and on them was stacked a pile of things good to look at and better to eat. The only reason the food did not immediately become part of the dozen fellows was because they were waiting with watering mouths for something to wash it down with. And this was being prepared as rapidly as Randolph and Ashley in the bedroom could do it. Perhaps they were trying to do it too rapidly, for Symington heard a voice exclaim, "Aw, look out, you ass, you're spilling it all over my bed."

While they were waiting, Dougal Davis and Reddy Armstrong and Harry Lawrence and Jim Linton and others came in. When the lounge, window-seat, chairs, tables, and coal-scuttle became crowded, the new-comers sat on the floor.

Presently the introductory strains of Mendelssohn's "Wedding March" came from the bedroom, followed by Randy and Dad Ashley and two assistants bearing aloft two basins, which seemed to be heavy. They strode in, swinging their feet far out in front in a stagey manner to the tune of the "Wedding March" which they shouted with their heads thrown back.

Hunter Ramsay jumped up and marched behind them. The rest thought this a good idea and did likewise, and all sang loud and stamped hard and made the poler growl in the room below, which did no good. Then after marching twice around the table they carefully set the bowls down at either end of it with the ice tinkling against the sides. One of the bowl-bearers remarked, "Maybe you don't think those things are heavy."

"Now then!" said Stehman the tackle, approaching the table. "Ah!" said Symington's friend Tucker. The others may have said things also. If they did not they looked them.

No one waited to be asked. Everyone was supposed to know without being told what was the object of white breasts of cold chicken with russet-brown skin, and rich Virginia ham with spices sticking in the golden-brown outside fat, and little, thin, home-made sandwiches and olives and jellies, Virginia jellies, you know, and beaten biscuit and chocolate cake and fruit cake, or black cake, as they call it in the South. As a matter of fact they all did seem to know, and this included Symington, who held his own with the others very well for a little prep. boy in training. He had forgotten to be sleepy now.

Thus began one of the greatest evenings in the life of Charlie Symington, and it lasted until two o'clock. It was an old-fashioned spread. There was no caterer with a gas-stove in the bedroom, or a table set with a bank of flowers down the centre, or properly attired waiters opening wine behind the chairs. Randolph's mother had sent up a lot of deliciously cooked stuff from the old place in Virginia. Randolph had said to some of the fellows, "I've got a box of grub. Can you come 'round this evening?" And by the looks of things most of them had found that they could as well as not.

Symington had the best time of them all, and, besides, he learned much. He noticed that quite as many fellows took lemonade as drank punch, and this was a matter of surprise to the prep. For his ideas of college men were largely drawn from would-be sportive young freshmen that drove through prep. school towns waving beer-bottles overhead and beating their horses into a gallop.

Nobody got drunk. Everyone became livelier and brighter and better, but that is the object of such gatherings, and those who confined their attentions to the lemonade end of the table were as noisy as the others. No one was urged to take the red fluid rather than the yellow. In fact no one observed which fellows visited which punch-bowl. No one but Symington. And he had been under the impression that at college a fellow's jaws were pried open with a baseball bat and rum was poured down his throat, while three other men held his legs and arms.

The room had now become beautifully hazy with smoke. Some of the fellows tipped their chairs back and put their feet up. The window-seat was full to overflowing. One man rested his head on another fellow's shoulder and asked him to muss his hair. The legs of the one having his hair mussed stretched out over the legs of two other fellows and intertwined with those of a third. Two men were sitting beside the oranges on the table. Some were on the floor with their backs against the wall. All had full stomachs and light jovial spirits. Symington was watching Dougal Davis blow rings.

Harry Lawrence started up "The Orange and the Black." They sang all the stanzas. Then they sang more songs, old songs which are still popular and new songs which were then popular and are now quite forgotten, probably. Everyone sang, whether he knew how or not. Symington sang too. The one he liked the best was a funny song beginning, "Oh, to-day is the day that he comes from the city." They sang that one over and over again. Then they sang it once more. They were all having a good time.

After a while the room became quiet and someone turned down the lights and they told ghost stories, which frightened the prep.

They wound up the evening by trooping downstairs in the dark, for the lights were turned out long ago, and marching up to the front campus, singing as they went. And there they danced about the cannon and sang and whooped and yelled until Bill Leggett came over with his lantern and said, in his gruff voice and good-natured manner, "Boys, it's nearly Sunday morning."

"All right, Bill," they answered. Then all said good-night and went to bed.

Tucker had a roommate some place, but Symington had his bedroom that night.

"If you want anything, just yell for me, Charlie. My room is right next, you know. Goodnight." Tucker was half undressed.

"I sha'n't want anything. Wait a minute, Tucker, please. I'm not sure about something, and it bothers me."

"Well?"

"Princeton won the football championship in '78, didn't we?"

"Say that again."

"Didn't we win in '78?"

"Yes, Charlie, we did."

Symington thought his friend Tucker was smiling at his ignorance. But that wasn't it.

THE MAN THAT LED THE CLASS

The Latin salutatory was finished. Dougal Davis bowed and took his seat and the applause began.

He had done well and he knew it, but he did not stop to dwell upon that now. There would be plenty of time to feel pleased with himself later on. At present his chief sensation was of jubilant relief at telling himself that the thing was over with at last.

Not many of his audience had understood much of what he had been saying, but that did not matter. The fellows smiled at the right time when he said something about *puellas pulchras*, and they nodded their heads knowingly when he made the reference to athletics, as he had told them beforehand to do. And he had gotten through without forgetting the paragraph beginning with "Postquam," as he feared he would.

He was mopping his good-looking brow. His nerves were still quivering, but he felt perfectly cool and unafraid of anything, and he sat very still with his eyes half closed, and felt the tension on his nerves soothingly relax. Then for the first time he heard the applause, and it occurred to him that all those many people out there were clapping their hands for him, and that for five minutes they had heard very little else but his voice, and he felt without glancing up that they were still looking at him and very likely thinking, "That is the man that led the class." He told himself all this with an inward smile of wonder at his own importance, and at his not being more impressed by it.

Then he slowly raised his eyes and moved his gaze around over the many fluttering fans to the right. He passed over it once without seeing it, then he found the face he was searching for. She was looking up at him with just the kind of a smile that he knew would be there, and when she caught his eye, the smile became radiant, and he fancied he saw a little look of triumph in it. This he answered with a shrug of his engowned shoulder and an almost imperceptible grimace, and quickly looked away again. No one else saw it, but she saw and she understood.

The applause had ceased, and the next man was introduced and the audience turned their attention to him.

Davis took a long breath and looked about him. There was a fat old lady fanning vigorously, and at every stroke of the fan a ray of light was reflected in his face. Over there on the right of the platform were the venerable trustees. Harry Lawrence's fine looking father, with the handsome head of gray hair, was in the front row, looking grave and indulgently interested. On the left were the faculty in their black gowns. They appeared more or less accustomed to all this. Down in front were his classmates, and back of these the many, many people closely crowded together. Their faces looked like little patches of white with dark marks for features, and nearly all of them seemed to be fanning.

He remembered the lining up under the elms this morning in front of North, and the band that played, and the girls that gazed, and the many classes calling "'82 this way!" and "'61 this way!" and the old-fashioned cheer that '79 gave. Then with the band taking a fresh hold on the air, how the long procession had begun its march under the trees toward the church, between the crowds of visitors who parted to either side and looked at them as they filed by.

First came that member of the faculty who is always grand marshal and carries an orange and black baton, then the august trustees followed by the faculty in their gowns and mortar boards, and behind these trooped the sons of Nassau; each class in the order of graduation, and last of all those who were about to become graduates, over whom all this fuss was being made, and who were somewhat impressed by it and by the length of their gowns.

He remembered the slow, dignified march led by the grand usher and his assistants up the aisle of the old church between the crowded pews of smiling fathers and proud mothers and the girls with bright-colored dresses. He recalled how amused and yet pleased he was at hearing a junior whisper to a girl beside him, "There he is—that's Davis, the one I was telling you about." This he remembered had interrupted the silent rehearsal of the sentence with the ablative absolute in it. But he did not have to rehearse it any more. All the salutatorian had to do was to sit still and hear what the other speakers had to say and feel good.

He was thinking about himself and the four years just past, and having a right good time at it. He recalled how he had been a nobody at the start, and he smiled as he remembered how some of these very fellows in the pews before him had looked down on him in freshman year, and how he had forced their respect and won their liking. He traced the progress of it from the first step when he gained the one freshman position on the *Princetonian* board and overheard someone say, "What! that poler?" up to the present time when people pointed him out on the campus and said, "There goes Dougal Davis." Few ambitious men graduate with as much to be proud of and as little to regret.

First there was the prize for leading the class in freshman year, then came the sophomore essay prize, and the Washington's birthday debate, and the next year a classical prize and two or three Hall honors, including one of the four appointments for the inter-Hall junior oratorical contest, in which he had won first place, and a number of other prizes of which he did not stop to think in detail, and finally the appointment as first representative of his Hall in the Lynde debate which had taken place the night before, and the result of which would be announced to-day. Intermingled with these were other honors, such as the membership of an elective club, and the presidency of his class in junior year, and the class oratorship on Class Day, and then the Latin salutatory to-day.

You see he had just about all one man could get, and before he left the room he was going to hear his name read out before everybody, as the winner of still a few more honors. This was the culmination of a rather successful career, and he told himself that he did not care how conceited it was, he was going to enjoy it for all it was worth, for before the sun set he would be an undergraduate no longer, and there would be plenty of time to find how small he was.

Dougal Davis was the son of a foreign missionary, and he had entered college with the intention of making a minister of the Gospel of himself. He still had that intention. He was one of the most popular men on the campus.

When he began his course he was as bristling with prejudices and as redolent of sanctimony as many high-minded young men of noble purpose and little tact, but unlike some of them he had sense of humor enough to find out pretty promptly that he was a young prig.

He soon shed many of his prejudices, and he was fair-minded enough to let the good wholesome atmosphere of the campus air out his sanctimony. This is a way of saying that early in freshman year he took himself in hand and decided that if he and a number of other fellows looked at a number of things in vastly different ways it did not necessarily follow that the other fellows were dead wrong. He was in evidence at class prayer-meetings, but not more than at the meetings at the lamp-post in front of Reunion, with his hands doubled up under a sweater, gossiping with the crowd. That is the sort of a fellow he was.

Davis's father had a small salary and a large family, like all missionaries, and one of the girls had come back to the States when Dougal did to go to a school in Philadelphia. So young Davis earned the price of his education.

But this was not so hard as it sounds. Being a minister's son he had a scholarship, which saved his tuition bills, and he ran a club, so that his board cost nothing. Leading the class in freshman year not only brought him the prize of $200, but the best kind of advertising with the faculty as well, so that in sophomore year he had more tutoring sent around to him than he knew what to do with. Then he became Princeton correspondent for several papers, and dropped tutoring except on special occasions and at very special rates. He had such a reputation that he could have had any price he asked. "Go to Davis; he can put you through any examination," they used to say.

In junior year he enlarged his newspaper correspondence and began doing some syndicate work. He gained a bit of reputation with football writing, and in his senior year he used to sign his name to a column of it every week. "The joke of it is," Dougal used to explain, "I don't know beans about the game." This was not strictly true, for no one with eyes could go through four years of tramping down to 'varsity field without absorbing enough to enlighten the average sporting editor.

In short, before Davis was three-quarters of the way through his college course, he was paying his expenses and making a surplus which was considerably larger than that which poor young men who earn their way through college to preach the Gospel are supposed to have.

Now he might have sent a portion of it out to his hard-working parents in Persia, or have helped to defray the expenses of his ambitious sister at school. This would have been noble of him, but he did nothing of the kind. One does not need much money in Persia; there's nothing to spend it on. His people had a large, comfortable home with a dozen servants to look after it, and they seemed to have leisure enough to write articles for English and American magazines now and then. A rich aunt looked out for his sister, and she had the reputation of dressing more artistically than any girl in the Walnut Street school. The only thing he did for her was to send an occasional box of candy, or a book, like any other brother. Davis did not even save his money. He blew it in on himself and his friends, like any other natural young man. What do you suppose he worked so hard for if it were not to go in with the rest of the club for coaches at Thanksgiving games, and to take runs to Philadelphia over Sunday, and to give spreads in his room on Saturday nights, and to do the other things for which one has sore need of money and for which he goes broke for about twenty days of each month? If Davis had been a modern undergraduate he would perhaps have spent money on good-looking clothes, though I hardly think that of him.

The only disadvantage in his way of living was that it took time, so that he did not have as much of it to loaf in as he would have liked. Especially as he was mixed up in half-a-dozen outside interests of the college world, and had a provokingly high stand in class to maintain besides. For although the fellows used to say he kept on leading his class from force of habit, as a matter of fact it took considerable valuable time.

The worst of it was that he had to do his reviewing up regularly week by week, for he was of no account at cramming all night for exams, he said. Perhaps this was true. When the crowd used to gather in half-undressed condition with wet towels around their heads and wild looks on their faces, Dougal generally stretched out upon the divan and drummed on a banjo, with his eyes half closed and a pipe in his mouth, and listened to the others quizzing and getting excited, and at twelve o'clock, except on rare occasions, he said good-night, and went to bed and slept like a child, and the next day would saunter into Examination Hall as fresh as a spring term Sunday, and write the best paper in the class. It is in this way that many fellows remember him best.

The reason he never seemed to be especially rushed was that he had the knack of arranging his time, and had learned while still in college that there are a great many moments in twenty-four hours. He went to breakfast before chapel, and he crammed a great deal into those odd hours that come between lectures, which most fellows spend in making up their minds what to do, and he found he better appreciated a loaf on Saturday night if he put in most of the daylight in work. It was in that way he managed to find time to keep up his Hall work and attend to his *Princetonian* duties and committee meetings and write orations and essays, besides managing one of the clubs and turning out an average of one thousand words of copy a day in time to catch the afternoon mail.

And it was in this way that he managed to keep from breaking down under it. When the bell in North struck five he always tossed aside his book and ran down the stairs three steps at a time and yelled, "Hello, Tommy Tucker," or "Billy Nolan," or somebody with all his might, and with him took a rattling hard walk—not down Nassau Street, but 'cross country—or else an hour's pull at the weights in the gymnasium with a cold shower-bath and a hard rub at the end of it, and then walked tingling with health and content to the club, when he ate the largest meal of anyone there—except when big Stehman was back from the training-table.

After this he stretched his legs far under the table and leaned his head against the back of the chair, and there lingered with the coffee and gossip, blowing beautiful smoke rings for an hour. He had been known to refuse a $5 tutoring offer for this hour, just as he had once sacrificed an elective course in Greek philosophy for the five o'clock one.

During the past year Davis had been making up his mind to a few things. One of them was that he would go out to the foreign field. He could not say that he felt himself called to it. He did not sign the pledge that was circulated about in the colleges at that time as the "Student volunteer movement."

Ever since he could remember he had intended to be a preacher, though there was a period, which came about the same time as his first pair of trousers, when he thought he would rather be a dragoman with a fierce mustache and big buttons. And now he came to the conclusion that he would become a foreign missionary, like his father.

He felt that he was pretty well suited to the work and would make a success of it. He had a strong constitution, a good voice, and adaptability to circumstances. He knew pretty well by nature how to get at people, and the summer spent slumming down in Rivington Street, New York, had taught him considerably more. Besides, he already had the language down fine, and could stumble along tolerably well with two of the low dialects.

What is more, he thought he would like it. He did not tell himself that it was noble to go and bury himself way out there, for there wasn't any burying about it. He liked the climate and expected to have a good time in Persia, with a man-servant to bow low and make his coffee in the morning, and to fill his big, long pipe every evening, and he pictured himself on a horse riding beside a certain blue river with peculiar big trees along the bank quite as often as saving souls.

At least this is the way he used to talk in pow-wows in fellows' rooms. But there were certain long-faced friends of his that misunderstood when he talked in this manner.

The salutatorian was not troubling himself about that just now, as he sat there on the stage resting his chin on one hand and fanning himself with a programme in the other. He had been idly listening to Nolan as he thundered and perspired about Purity in Politics. For his part he preferred gamey Billy Nolan, the all-round athlete, to earnest William the orator. Nervous little poler Stacy was now straining his lungs with his well-committed plea for the Greek Ideal. Davis was not following it very closely. He glanced down at his classmates in the front rows. He knew that before the day was over he was going to feel pretty sad. That was not troubling him very much now either. But every time he looked down there a certain thing bobbed up and spoiled the pleasant taste in his mouth. It was hardly worth getting uncomfortable over. This was the way it had begun, long ago last fall, as they sat around the table after dinner talking football. And you can see how ridiculous it was to worry about it.

Davis was holding forth at some length with considerable earnestness, as he had a perfect right to do, of course, and Jim Linton had not joined in the discussion. He seldom did. He was quietly sipping his coffee at the end of the table and looking quizzically interested.

Presently he interrupted. "Oh, Dougal," he said. He had arisen to go and was refilling his pipe.

Dougal stopped short. "Yes?" he said in an intense tone.

Linton looked at him a moment, folded up his pouch, put it in his pocket, and struck a match.

Then he said, between puffs, "I'd a little rather you would not get excited, Dougal," and started off for the billiard-room.

It was nothing but a bit of ordinary club chaff such as passes back and forth every day, and Linton forgot the occurrence before he finished chalking his cue. But Dougal's cheeks had flushed crimson, and before he knew what he was saying he had come out with a muttered remark in which the word "gentleman" was loud enough for all at the table to hear, and that is a very awkward word to handle sometimes.

That was the reason no one said anything for a moment. Silences were rare in that room. He did not go on with the discussion of the defective coaching system. Nor did the others.

A little later as he started for the campus old Jack Stehman joined him and said, in his sober, conscientious way, "Say, Dougal, you had no business saying what you did about Jimmy. Of course you didn't mean it, but you had better apologize, don't you think?"

Davis said he did not look at it in that way, and changed the subject. Before he got to sleep that night he saw what a fool he had made of himself, and made up his mind to apologize to Linton before the whole table. But that was in the middle of the night.

The next day there were guests at the club. The following day Linton dined out. The day after that Davis tried to make himself do it as they sat about the fireplace, but he postponed it until some time when his heart was not beating so loud, for he did not feel himself called upon to make a scene before the whole club. When he thought over what he meant to say it all seemed very ridiculous, and he blushed at the thought of it. Linton of all fellows would dislike any slopping over of this sort. So he changed his mind and decided to speak to Linton alone about it.

But it was a very hard thing for a man like Davis to talk to a man like Linton about a thing like this. There was something about Linton that he did not understand. He was the one man that made him self-conscious. He always felt as though Linton saw through him and understood how ambitious he was, and was laughing at him for his strenuous struggling. He told himself that he did not propose to be in awe of a lazy dilettante who thought himself a clever reader of human nature. But that did not help him to apologize. And the longer he put it off the harder it became, naturally. And the longer he put it off the more he found to dislike in Linton, which was also natural, only you would not have thought this of Davis.

After a while he began wondering how he had taken to Linton in the first place, and why the other fellows liked him so much. Every time they were together he began comparing himself with him. By most standards Davis ought to have been satisfied. Linton himself never seemed to think of comparison. He seemed to calmly take it for granted that Dougal was a wonderful man, and often referred to it as an acknowledged fact. He seemed to be glad to speak of it. But he had a way of making fellows love him that was galling to the man that led the class.

All the college bowed down to Dougal Davis; not twenty under-classmen knew who Linton was. But Timberly and Reddy Armstrong and Jack Stehman had a way of throwing an arm about lazy Linton, whom they loved, that it did not occur to them to do with the wonderful Dougal Davis, whom they admired. Davis wanted that love. He wanted everything. You see he had quite a disposition to contend with.

So he kept on having disagreeable times with himself and the conscience which would not let up. Finally he made up his mind to patch it all up on Commencement Day, and he had hit upon a plan by which he could make just amends to Linton, he told himself, and duly punish himself at the same time, and then he could graduate in peace.

Meanwhile he would have to stop thinking about that and walk down from the stage with the other Commencement speakers, for Charles Benjamin Howard had finished telling people about the Utility of Difference, and the orchestra was playing "Ta-ra-ra boom de ay."

There was an intermission of ten minutes now. After that would come the announcement of prizes and the conferring of degrees, then Smith's valedictory, followed by the benediction, and then the class would walk out into the world with their little diplomas under their arms tied with pretty ribbons.

The audience changed their positions and looked about at the other people there, whispered to each other, and went to fanning again. Some of the fathers looked at their watches and yawned and wished Commencement was over with behind their programmes, and fell to thinking about things in the office which they had come here to forget.

Other old grads. smiled kindly, and remembered how they used to do when they were in college. The young alumnus looked pityingly at the graduating class in the front rows and thought how little these boys knew about the big world he knew so much of.

Meanwhile the juniors and the lower classmen were very active and noisy in the rear of the old church. The Whig men were gathering on the left-hand side, and Clio Hall on the right. Many reinforcements were arriving that had not been near the church during the other exercises. The aisles became jammed. The seats were already so.

Suddenly a man jumped up on a pew, and screamed, "Now, fellows! Clio Hall, this way! Hip-hip!"

"Clio Hall—this way!" came out with startling force from many throats.

This woke everyone up, and those that had never been there before were a little shocked for a moment. The loud voices echoed strangely against the old walls and among the old pillars and under the old galleries, which by the way are used to all this and weren't surprised a bit. No doubt they miss it these days.

Then the left-hand side of the church raised its voice and said, "Whig Hall, this way! Whig Hall this wa-ay!" in still fiercer tones. Then Clio called itself together again, and then Whig Hall cheered and so did Clio, and gave a long cheer and so did Whig. Then both cheered for themselves at once, and tried to drown each other out, and succeeded. They kept this up until time was called. That is, the clerk of the board of trustees arose and stretched his long neck and began to announce the prizes from a long list in his hand. This was interesting.

Whenever he read out an award in his strong voice, it was met with a tremendous cheer from the Hall whose member won the prize. It mattered not whether the honor was one for which a literary society's training could count; they cheered anyway, whether it was a fellowship in modern languages or a prize in the School of Science draughtsmanship. Nor did it matter whether the man had never since the first week after his initiation worked the combination lock of the Hall door. They cheered him anyway. And when the two societies were in doubt as to which he belonged to, they both cheered. It made magnificent noise.

There are a great many of these prizes. One has no idea until Commencement comes that there are so many advertised in the catalogue; and the clerk read each one out in a loud voice, and then waited for the cheering to cease.

Dougal Davis had heard his name announced three times, and each time the cheer rang out from the enthusiastic throng in the rear he felt the little echoing thrill inside of him.

Once as he stepped down from the platform he caught a glimpse of a man leading the cheer for him. The man's back was turned, but he saw him standing there 'way up on the railing of the pew in his excitement, and he saw his arms vigorously jerking out the cheer.

Davis was used to this sort of thing and he held his features very well, though as he marched up for the third time he felt rather foolish, for the audience were smiling audibly at the sight of Dougal Davis, of Persia, running off with so many prizes. Timberly asked him when he came down, "Why don't you stay up there, Dougal? I'd sit on the edge platform and swing my legs."

It was only at the announcement of the Lynde prize debate that he felt at all tremulous. His friends kept telling him that he was sure of it, but he felt that he would not get it. This is, as everyone knows, the greatest inter-Hall prize offered, and many people consider it the greatest honor of a college lifetime. It was quite enough for a fellow to feel weak at the stomach over. Dougal kept repeating under his breath, "What's the difference, what's the difference?" and he reminded himself that there were a second and a third prize as well as the first, and that any way, even if he won none of them, it was a pretty fine thing to have secured the appointment from his Hall. Besides, he was doing so many things that he could afford to drop an honor or two.

"The Lynde Prize Debate," came in the resonant tones of the tall, gaunt clerk. Everything was very still.

The cheerers were silent. The two leaders were standing on tip-toe, each with his elbows doubled up and mouth half open, ready to begin the cheer. One of them, however, would have to keep still. Dougal shut his lips.

"First prize awarded to Dougal Davis, of Pers——"

Then came the loud, eager "'Ray! 'Ray! 'Ray!'" of the quick cheer, and then two more quick ones, and next a long one with "Davis!" on the end, then the word "Davis! Davis! Davis!" that way, three times. Then they began giving more quick cheers again and a few long ones, as if they had just started.

Meanwhile the clerk kept his sober gaze upon the paper in his hand, waiting to announce the second and third winners and pretending to be annoyed at the delay, though enjoying it as much as any girl in the audience.

"Good work, Dougal, good work," cried one of the four fellows pounding him on the back.

Dougal did not smile slightly or look unconcerned. He grinned all over his face and enjoyed it. As soon as the attention was taken away from him he leaned back in the corner of the pew and enjoyed it some more. That is the way to do.

He was still tense and excited from his victory when a few minutes later he heard the clerk reading off something about the new fellowship in Political Science. This was the one he had gone in for, and he had felt doubtful over the result, because he had not been able to spend as much time upon it as he wanted to, and it required a great deal. However, the only other man in the race was nothing to be afraid of. But all the same a little dart of dread shot through him now, and he thought what if he should lose it after all. It would not do at all. This was what he wanted more than any of the honors. He had a particular reason for wanting to win it. This he failed to do.

Before he was quite aware of what was taking place the clerk had already made the announcement and the crowd were wildly cheering, cheering that other fellow as if they had never heard of Dougal Davis. He felt like a man that steps off a bridge in the dark; he heard the splash and felt a shock, but he did not know just what had happened. He had never been beaten in anything before. It came very hard. But that was not what made it hurt so much. It was because Linton had won it.

He could not help thinking of the little speech he had planned to make that evening—"Well, you see, Jimmie, I haven't time for it, anyway. I have to go to the Seminary, and maybe to the Medical College after that. So I thought I would resign, and I hope you'll apply for it and come back to the old place for another year. You're sure to get it, if you apply for it." Wasn't it a pretty little speech?

He turned and glanced over at Linton, who sat with his head nestled contentedly against Reddy Armstrong's shoulder, while the happy-looking fellows all around him were punching and pounding him and rumpling up his hair as if they never would cease; and as if they were glad Dougal Davis was beaten. Linton himself only raised his eyebrows and shook his head deprecatingly. He seemed to take it all very easily, as if he were accustomed to winning prizes and beating Dougal Davis, and he still wore that imperturbable look, and Davis knew that it would have been just as imperturbable and contented looking if he had lost.

And this spoiled the salutatorian's day of triumph. He did not glance back now to where his sister and aunt were sitting. He forgot to unroll his sheepskin as the others did when they came down from the stage with them. He blew his breath through it against the palm of his hand and looked absent-mindedly at the scratched paint of the old-fashioned pew. He remained thus all through Smith's valedictory, except once when the speaker stretched out both arms and the class arose; then he listened for a moment and said, "Biff!" under his breath. When it was all over he passed out with his class and through the gazing throng, thinking not of the much that he had won, but only of the one thing he had lost, and this was unfortunate, because much people were looking at him and thinking how fine it was to be Davis, and that is fame, and it was too bad to miss it.

Linton had no ambition and he colored meerschaum beautifully. He was usually mum in a crowd, but he was fine company on a long cross-country walk, and he knew more about ordering a dinner than any man on the campus, except one of the faculty.

When he did not want you in his room he told you so, and he was the kind of a fellow you would do anything for after you came to know him.

He had a very efficient sense of humor, which does not mean that he said funny things at the table. Some people thought him sarcastic. But many fellows went to him for advice or sympathy, and it was not only because he could keep his mouth absolutely closed.

Linton had a walking acquaintance with every road, lane, and pathway within a radius of twenty miles of the campus. He knew how long it took to cover any route, and where there were good places to stop and rest, especially the quaint ones where they served it in mugs.

Here he used to sit and sip and smoke the golden afternoon away, dreaming of how it all must have been years ago in the old stage coach days when the horses drew up on the clattering cobble-stones and the passengers alighted and looked about and asked how many more miles it was, and the red-faced driver jumped down from the box and swaggered into the tap-room, and called for a pint of ale, and told the landlord how bad the pike was near New Brunswick.

He considered himself somewhat of an artist. There were ever so many bits that he was fond of showing you if he thought you could appreciate them; like the bend in the canal up toward Baker's basin, with peculiar water and willow-coloring in springtime. Linton said it was like a French water-color. He used to carry a gun over his shoulder, and say he was going snipe-shooting; really it was to look for things like this, and get up a big appetite for dinner. He could also point out a view of gentle hills and rolling green fields on the way to Kingston that was a good imitation of English landscape, he said, and he knew just where the tower of the School of Science ought to make an effect through treetops, like the view of

Magdalen tower from a point in Addison's walk, if it were only beautiful Gothic instead of ugly Renaissance. But perhaps all this was merely to show that he had once canoed down the Thames from Oxford to London.

He was very well up in the ancient history of the town, also. He knew all about most of the old houses, and he had sketches of the best of the old brass-knockers and colonial doorways. It is said that he used to prowl about on moonlight nights for this purpose. Small window-panes were another thing he was insane over. He had substituted for the ordinary panes of his windows, dingy little square ones with thick frames painted black. Some of the fellows said the reason he did this was to be odd. Linton blew smoke, and said yes, that was the reason.

But it was the old campus that he loved the most. He knew just about all there was to find out about it, and dreamed a great deal more.

He had ever so many favorite aspects, such as the one of the back of the Dean's house—with small, square window-panes—from away over at a point between Whig and Clio Halls, and the rear view of Prospect across the stretch of sloping meadow toward the canal, and a number of congenial little spots that meant something to him, like the stone buttress at the bottom of the tower of Witherspoon, a great place to warm your back against in spring sunshine, with the blue smoke trickling lazily from your mouth and the fellows batting up flies on the old diamond; and then for midnight chats there were the smooth steps of chapel with the elms saying things in low tones overhead. But those midnight chats were all over now. It was Commencement Day, and it was the saddest thing that had ever happened to Linton.

He was not at all anxious to spring forth into the world and battle with opportunity and all the other things that the class-day speakers and the valedictorian said that he was going to do. He thought this little world was good enough for him, and there wasn't much spring in him.

Ever since he could read he had been told that youth was the happiest time in life, and he had come to the conclusion that it must be so. He did not like the idea of giving it up. He had become well settled where he was, and had just gotten rid of a persistent siege of kid-pessimism—of which he was now very much ashamed—and was just beginning to realize what a big, beautiful, real thing friendship was, and now—Jack and Timber and Billy and Red, where would they all be in three days' time? It seemed pretty sudden, this thing of breaking up.

And there was very little comfort to him in the thought of coming back next year. What would the old place be without the old class. He did not like to think about it.

It struck the class as a pretty joke for Jimmie Linton to bob up and win a fellowship. "How did you happen to do it?" said Tucker, on the way out of church. "I didn't know you had any brains."

"Didn't you?" said Linton; "I've quite a lot of them. And I worked like a good little boy for that fellowship; but nobody will give me any credit for it. They all know that if Dougal hadn't been too busy with other things, I would have had no show." He was quite right. There was nothing modest in this. Dougal Davis had about as good powers of acquisition as anyone graduated since the time of Aaron Burr.

Political science was not strictly in Linton's line. He wrote things for the Lit., and elected all the English courses. He was a great browser in Elizabethan literature, and when he dabbled in verse this was evident. One of the exchanges once called him a nineteenth century Herrick. Linton felt right pleased, and wrote something nice about the University of Virginia man that said it in the next Lit., and also made it an excuse to give one of his famous spreads. You would have expected him to go in for an English fellowship, if for any. But he did not go in for any deliberately. He was not in the habit of studying his courses more than enough to get through the examinations, except when he ran across something he was interested in, or a professor he liked. There are many excuses for laziness.

In Political Economy, and such subjects, he liked the lecturer very much, and he found himself becoming interested in the primitive man, and the origin of society, and all that. The farther he went in the course, the more interested he became. He went to the library, and often walked past the Elizabethan alcove. Next he began buying the books, because he liked to feel that he owned them, and rub them up against his cheek, and he soon had a shelf full of Bagehot and big, thick Sir Henry Maine and others.

Then because he had never done anything serious during his course, and because he knew it would please his people and amuse the fellows, he announced his intention of trying for the Political Science fellowship. There was no one else in for it.

He went about it scientifically, and was surprised to find how much enthusiasm he had aroused in himself. He had never known before what a fine thing study was. He said he wished he had done more of it during his college course.

He was surprised when he heard a few weeks later that Dougal Davis was in the field. Historical work he thought was still further out of Davis's line. But he only rolled over on the divan and went on reading. For he argued thus: "I like this stuff and I don't see how it can hurt me to learn a lot about something. If I don't fetch a fellowship I won't have to correct examination papers. I'd hate to correct examination papers."

One day at the club he asked Dougal—he sat opposite—what he wanted with political science. Davis cleared his throat and said every preacher of modern times should know something of sociology, which was undoubtedly true. But that was not the reason. And somehow Linton guessed it.

It was twilight and the class had gathered together on the steps of Old North for their last senior singing. Only they were no longer seniors; it was "by and by" now, and they were out in the "wide, wide world." They huddled up close together as if half frightened at the thought of its being the last time.

There were but few undergrads. stretched out under the elms to listen, and most of these were the juniors—seniors they were now—waiting to rapaciously take possession of the steps the moment the present occupants marched off for their last supper together at nightfall. These and a handful of the out-of-town visitors were all that were left of the big Commencement crowds that had been gathering there every evening to hear the seniors sing. Sometimes they had felt that they would have preferred being left a little more to themselves, if it were possible, during the last days of college life.

But now this unmolested aloneness only added to their dreariness and made them feel the ghastly certainty of this evening's being the end of all. The grass was trampled and faded, and the crowd that had trodden it was gone. The bell in Old North belfry rang out painfully loud.

"Well, fellows, let's sing," said the leader, rising slowly. He raised his chin and then bobbed his head and started up, "The Orange and the Black," just as they had all seen him do many times before.

They sang as they had never sung before. It did not matter what were the words of the song. "They stole his wallet, they stole his staff," had nothing in it that was especially apropos of college friendships or the sadness of farewell, but the way they sang it, with the long-drawn "Ramski Ho," meant something. It was so full of association. And no one noticed this time whether the man behind him was on a key of his own. His only thought was, "When shall I hear Billy's good old bark again after to-night?" And when Sam's and when Ed's and Big Hill's and Little Hill's and where would be the fellow a year from now whose shoulder was next to his own.

During the past month or two the class of Ninety Blank had been drawn very close together by the thought of what was coming. They had never been very seriously cliqued up, but what there was of dissension was forgotten, and they were now one solid crowd. Fellows who had never anything to do with each other before except to say, "Hello, there, Ray!" and "Hello, Harry!" had taken to strolling around the campus together arm-in-arm talking about what they were going to do next year and wondering why they had never happened to see more of each other in the past, and regretting that there were to be no opportunities for doing so in the future.

But during the excitement of Commencement week, with the crowds of old grads. and of girls and the big baseball game and the concerts and Class Day full of its exhibition farewells in the church and around the cannon, and the teas and the big dance on Tuesday night, and the many other things that filled up every moment of every day and night—together with the responsibility of seeing to the entertainment of their guests—all this, and the feeling of importance at being the cause of so much color and sound had in a measure distracted their minds from the thought of what it all meant. But now all that was changed.

The last of the display ceremonies was finished. The class had their diplomas. It was all over. The rollicking old grads. with their many reunions and their old-fashioned cheers and their funny songs had left for the city and business again for a year. The girls and their mothers and their parasols had vanished like the chinese lanterns among the trees. The campus was almost deserted, and except for their own voices, was as still as a cemetery. Each man on the steps was realizing as he never had done before how glad had been those four years, and how startlingly fast they had sped by, and how much more these friends of his meant to him than he had ever imagined friends could mean.

Two of the number had been obliged to pack their trunks and depart during the afternoon without waiting for the banquet. The whole class were at the station to see them off. They did it in the old-fashioned way, with much cheering and singing, and the old custom of lifting them up and putting them through the car windows. Then after each man had shaken the hands of those departing, and said, "God bless you, Tommy," they had watched while the little train rolled down the grade and became smaller and smaller, and they cheered until the two men waving their hats on the rear platform were hidden behind the curve. Then they marched solemnly back across the campus again, and tried to go on with the packing of their own trunks.

But few had been able to remain very long in the lonely, old, familiar dens. There were too many things to suggest the old times which sent big wedges into throats, and they realized that there were to be few enough opportunities of being with those fellows out under the trees to waste time in dreary packing. "It's too deuced hot up there in my room," said Harry Lawrence to Billy Nolan.

For the most part they had spent the afternoon in silent, moody wanderings, in groups of twos and fours and half dozens, all about the old, dear, familiar landmarks of the campus. Now at evening they were gathered together as a body again. This was to be the last time. And that thought kept recurring to each man on the steps.

It was about dusk now. The front campus was wrapped in that strange half-glow that sometimes comes at late senior singing time. It was very much in keeping with other elements of the scene, and it had its effect upon the fellows.

Old North seemed solemn and dignified, but somehow more gentle and caressable than formerly. Even the old elms, who have seen this thing happen so many, many times, ceased whispering for a space and listened. John, the college policeman, left Reunion for his home down William Street, and Sam, the night watchman, said, "Good-night, John," and took his place. Bill Leggett took down his lantern and started around to light the campus lamps as he always did at this hour. The village street seemed far off, and its lights and its bit of life seemed part of another world. There was a pause in the singing.

It lasted a long time. Tucker scratched a match on the stone steps. The crack seemed very loud. Those near by turned and watched him light his pipe and watched him throw the match to the ground. It kept on burning for a little while. They watched it until it went out.

Presently Doc. Devereaux, the leader, said, "Fellows, there are a lot of chairs and benches scattered about. Let's drag them up here in front of the steps and make a circle." They all arose and did it as if it had been a command.

The rattling of the chairs against each other sounded harsh and discordant, and yet no one seemed to want to lessen it. Some of the fellows laughed and joked a little, as though they weren't thinking of anything serious. It made a large circle. They sat down in comparative silence. The Class President arose and said, "Say, fellows, let's sing 'Here's to you, my jovial friend,' all around the class, and each man stand up while we're singing to him."

They started with the President and went around to the left. You know that drinking song. It's a simple little salute, but there's more heart in its swelling high notes than in anything ever written. But perhaps that is because of its association.

"Here's to you, Jack Stehman," they sang.

"Here's to you, my jovial friend,

And we'll drink with all our heart,

For sake of company—

We'll drink before we part,

Here's to you, Jack Stehman."

Stehman, the President, had arisen when his name was called, and remained standing while the song was carried through. The big fellow seemed to loom up bigger than ever in the half dark. He arose with his old, well-known slouch, and the sight of this little characteristic brought up to every one of them the whole big, lovable personality of the man.

He started to look around at the fellows and smile as they began to sing, but the clear, warm notes rang out, "We'll drink before we part," and he changed his mind and looked down at the grass under his feet. He was not embarrassed. He merely preferred looking down. It was so different from Class Day, when he had made his much-applauded President's address, and told people in his nice set speech about the sadness of farewell and the beauty of the elms. He was the one all the girls had asked the most questions about. The class censor had guyed him about his brand new dignity and his good looks. Nobody was feeling like guying him now.

Little Stacy sat next. He did not stand up very high. There was not much to him. He had been a poler all through the course, and you would not have expected the thing to affect him very much, but you could see his thin hands working nervously along the edge of his coat as he looked about at the half-darkened crowd of faces, and he smiled his foolish, little, self-conscious smile. The little chap had no idea that they would ever sing to him in that way, and when he heard Harry Lawrence's strong bass come out with "And we'll drink with all our heart," he fairly quivered. When he sat down the President reached a big arm about him.

Then came Reddy Armstrong. He was not very tall either. He stood up very straight and stiff with his round, freckled face screwed up into funny twists. He only stared straight ahead into nothing. He looked dazed. He was dazed. He had been through some very queer things that day. "Poor little Red," thought Linton as he looked at him.

All around the big circle went the song until it ended with Timberly, who sat on Stehman's right. By this time it was too dark to see Timberly's queer features. Perhaps it was just as well.

"Now," said the President, simply, "let's all cross hands and sing 'Auld Lang Syne.' Doc., start it up, please."

They arose, and each man gave his right-hand comrade his left hand, and his left-hand comrade his right, and they sang the good old song in the good old way, with the clasped hands swinging far up and down in time to the music.

Presently the song was finished. It seemed to stop suddenly. They all waited a moment in silence to see whether the leader had another verse to begin.

But he did not. Jack Stehman stepped out into the middle of the ring. "Now, fellows," he said, "let's give three good rousing cheers for the dear old class—God bless every man in it—and then we'll give up the steps to the juniors—the seniors I mean—and march four abreast to the dinner. Are you ready? Hip! hip! ... another one—Hip! hip!"

Linton was standing apart over beside the steps. His back was turned toward the others.

While the rest were cheering, Dougal Davis crossed over to him.

"Jim," he said, "I haven't congratulated you yet on winning the fellowship."

Linton kept on looking at the newly planted class ivy. His hands were in his pockets and his legs spread apart.

"Did you notice that I hadn't, Jim?"

Linton turned around suddenly. "Oh, yes, I noticed it. But that was this morning." He put his hand on Davis's shoulder as in junior year.

"Shut up, Dougal," he said; "we haven't any time to waste in talk."

"All right," said Dougal. "Don't let's be left behind. They are starting." He laughed a little. It was a foolish-sounding laugh. Linton did not observe that. He laughed also, in very much the same way.

They stepped in line with the others and marched off the campus singing, with all their might,

"Nassau! Nassau! Ring out the chorus free.

Nassau! Nassau! Thy jolly sons are we.

Care shall be forgotten, all our sorrows flung away,

　　　While we are marching thro' Princeton."